The Realtor & Home Owner's Guide to

Short Sales

Step by Step

Loren K. Keim

Copyright © 2009 by Loren K. Keim

All rights reserved. No part of this book shall be reproduced or transmitted in any form or by any means, electronic, mechanical, magnetic, photographic including photocopying, recording or by any information storage and retrieval system, without prior written permission of the publisher. No patent liability is assumed with respect to the use of the information contained herein. Although every precaution has been taken in the preparation of this book, the publisher and the author assume no responsibility for errors or omissions. Neither is any liability assumed for damages resulting from the use of the information contained herein.

ISBN 978-1442120808

Table of Contents

Table of Contents 3
Introduction and Disclaimer 7
Chapter 1: Why is America in Financial Chaos? 9
   A Little History about Mortgages and Home
   Ownership 11
   Was Lending Money to Everyone Good or Bad?
   18
Chapter 2: Understanding the Options 23
   A Foreclosure Story 24
   People in Tough Situations 26
   The Options when facing Foreclosure 29
      Foreclosure by Judicial Sale 30
      Foreclosure by Power of Sale 31
      Owner's Right of Redemption 32
   The Seven Options to Avoid Foreclosure 32
      Mortgage Modification 34
      Forbearance Agreement 36
      Repayment Plan 37
      Re-instatement of Mortgage 38
      Short Sale 39
      Deed in Lieu of Foreclosure 39
      Bankruptcy 40
   Why bother avoiding foreclosure? 41
   The Risk of Waiting Too Long 43
   The Four Options in a "Need to Move" Situation
   45
      Renting the Home 45
      Deed in Lieu of Foreclosure 47
      Short Sale 48

Summary 48
Chapter 3: The Risks and Rewards of Short Sales 51
  Pros of short sale 51
  Cons of short sale 53
Chapter 4: The Short Sale – Step by Step 57
  Step 1: Contact Your Lender for Information... 58
  Step 2: Market Your Property and Find a Buyer
  60
  Step 3: Negotiating an Agreement 61
    Arm's Length Transactions 63
    Risk of Selling with a Short Sale: Full
    Disclosure 63
    Addendum to Sale's Contract 66
  Step 4: Put Together a Short Sale Package for
  your Lender 68
  Step 5: Start Calling the Lender! 85
    What if there's more than one mortgage? 88
    Negotiating with Junior Liens 92
    Getting to Settlement 94
Chapter 5: Realtor's guide to growing their business
through short sales 95
  Benefits for working short sales 96
  Challenges of working with short sales 97
  Prospecting for Short Sales 99
    Prospecting at the Courthouse 101
    Cold Calling Clients 107
    Advertising for Clients 109
    Attracting Customers with Workshops 111
    Word of Mouth 112
    Follow Up 113
    Testimonial Letters 115
  The Short Sale Listing Appointment 116

- 4 -

Answering the Home Owner's Objections 120
Protecting Yourself with Disclosures 126
   Summary 128
Other Books by Loren Keim 131
Order online at 131
How to Sell Your Home in Any Market: 6 Reasons Why Your Home Isn't Selling... and What You Can Do to Fix Them. (Sphinx Legal) 131
Glossary 135
Index 143

Introduction and Disclaimer

    This book is intended primarily to assist home owners and Realtors in understanding the options to avoid foreclosure and the process of selling a home using the technique known as a "short sale". A short sale occurs when a lender agrees to release a property from a mortgage to be sold and settled despite the fact that the lender is owed more than they are receiving in the transaction. Because each of the 50 states and the District of Columbia has differing systems of foreclosure, the book takes a broad look at the process of how short sales work, including the steps to applying for and negotiating a short sale.

    What this book is *not* is legal advice or tax advice. My suggestion is that if you are considering selling your home and you owe more than it can currently be sold for in today's real estate market, or if you are a Realtor advising a client of their possibilities, you should seek legal and tax advice.

    If you are a home owner, weigh whatever a Realtor, attorney and tax advisor tell you, and make your decision once you are fully informed. In many cases, a short sale may be your best opportunity to avoid having a bankruptcy or foreclosure on your credit, which could impact you for many years to come.

    Keep in mind, however, that a Realtor makes money if you sell your home rather than obtaining a loan modification from your lender or a forbearance agreement from your lender. Likewise, an attorney makes money if you file a foreclosure rather than performing a short sale through a Realtor. Before the huge and powerful attorney and realtor lobbies come down on me, I'm simply explaining that you have to be careful of the advice you receive.

Chapter 1:
Why is America in Financial Chaos?

Why are so many Americans in such financial trouble? How many homes will end up in foreclosure by the time the economic crisis has ended? How can we, as a country, pull out of this nosedive? Experts around the country have been debating this situation since early 2008. What's clear is that the crisis is a complex issue and resolving it won't be easy or done quickly.

The real estate market, and the broader economy, is cyclical. We all know it, and we've all heard it. Life is a rollercoaster ride and at times it goes up and at times it goes down. In May of 2006, I was on a stage in front of hundreds of real estate agents, appraisers, and local professionals at Lehigh University in

Bethlehem, Pennsylvania. I was attempting to forecast the coming real estate market. My belief was that the fundamentals of the economy were fairly solid, but that prices had risen too fast in comparison with income levels and that the market would have to slow down, and possibly shrink.

In the presentation, I likened the coming decline a slow leak in a balloon that would hopefully have a soft landing. Obviously, in hindsight, we all see that the balloon has been riddled with bullets, grenades, and a few missiles. During the presentation, a mortgage broker, Robert Wilfinger, pointed out that we weren't accounting for the huge number of subprime loans that he believed would be foreclosed, which, he believed, would lead to a sharp decline in home values. He also explained that the mortgage industry had become too lax. Lenders were giving loans to virtually anyone who could breathe.

Part of the reason that lenders were giving loans so freely was a change in policy in Washington that eased restrictions on lending in order to assist more families in owning their own homes instead of renting. While this was a noble cause, it was not the best use of our financial system and is one of the primary reasons that we're in this historic decline.

"*But Loren*," you may ask, "*what does this have to do with me? I can't pay my mortgage because I lost my job. I don't really care about this whole subprime thing. I had a normal mortgage.*"

You can't sell the house because it's worth less than you paid for it in 2006. It's worth less because the mortgage market has collapsed, making it more difficult to get mortgages and driving real estate prices down. The mortgage market has collapsed because our government and many other governments made decisions based on "feel good" politics rather than making sensible decisions. I've included this section because I am a firm believer that history repeats itself. At this point in time, we are passing stimulus packages and housing packages to try to correct the symptoms, but ignoring the real fundamental problems. If I can explain to you what I now believe happened, hopefully somewhere down the road we'll be better prepared to avoid the next catastrophic real estate loss.

A Little History about Mortgages and Home Ownership

In 1990, approximately 64.2% of Americans owned their own homes. Lenders carefully selected who would receive mortgages based on a few key indicators of their ability to repay the loans. In the real estate industry, we called these indicators the four "C's". They include:

- **Credit Worthiness**. If the borrower doesn't have a decent credit score, it shows they have not paid their bills on time. If the borrower isn't paying their bills now, what would make a lender believe they will get better at paying them once they own a home?

- **Capital**. In business, it's called having skin-in-the-game. Lenders don't want to loan the entire amount of a purchase, because the buyer or borrower doesn't have anything invested in the purchase. If their situation changes, it is easier for the buyer or borrower to walk away because they don't have anything to really lose, other than their credit rating.

- **Collateral**. The home simply has to be worth what the buyer is paying for it. A lender doesn't want to risk having to take back a property and re-sell it if there isn't enough equity to sell the home in the case of default.

❑ **Capacity.** The borrower has to have an income that allows them to make the payments. Lenders carefully determined whether or not the borrower could make the payments by assessing how long the borrower had been employed and what percentage of their income could be used to make the mortgage payment.

This system of carefully screening candidates for mortgages worked effectively in keeping the number of foreclosures very low for most of the last century. During the 1990's, the Community Reinvestment Act (CRA) was used to pressure lenders to reduce restrictions on the qualifications of buyers in order to increase the number of home owners, and particularly to assist minorities and low-income home buyers in purchasing homes. In fact, in 1999, the New York Times reported "that Fannie Mae and Freddie Mac were under pressure from the Clinton administration to increase lending to minorities and low-income home buyers"[1]

During the beginning of his administration, the 1992 Housing Bill set a goal for Fannie Mae and Freddie Mac to have 30% of their home loans be made to low and moderate income households. In 1996, that number was raised to 40% and then raised again to 42% in 1997.[ii] The GSEs then gave preferential treatment to mortgage companies and lenders who reduced their underwriting criteria. Countrywide Financial Corp. was the first to sign HUD's "Declaration of Fair Lending Principals and Practices."[iii]

All this boils down to the fact that these quasi-government institutions were the largest buyer of loans, and they actively reduced the restrictions required for obtaining a mortgage. Most lenders followed suit in order to take advantage of writing more loans and selling them to these institutions.

Programs became available, through Fannie Mae and Freddie Mac lenders and through Subprime lenders, offering 100% financing, 103% financing and in some cases, up to 125% financing. The supposed logic behind this idea was that buyers had decent credit and stable jobs but weren't able to save any money, so why not loan them the entire amount? Unfortunately, it also means that these home buyers had little or no money put into the property, and therefore, little to lose by walking away. It also left no equity for a lender if the buyer defaulted on the mortgage.

Even that wasn't enough. Programs were created that allowed borrowers to state their income on applications rather than actually provide proof of their earnings. In this case, the logic was that self employed people didn't show all their income, or couldn't prove it readily, so these individuals could not be turned away from being approved for a mortgage. The lender would simply charge them a slightly higher interest rate than the norm for the privilege of "stating" their income.

Lower and lower credit requirements continued to push the pool of potential home buyers into the depths of unqualified individuals. The checks and balances of the mortgage industry were totally out of whack with reality. Low interest rates, combined with low or no down payments and easy credit with very few verifications is a recipe for mortgage disaster.

In many cases across the country, there were lenders who were conservative and unwilling to follow these new reduced guidelines. Some of these banks and mortgage companies were sued by community action groups claiming they were discriminating against segments of the population based on archaic rules. Most lenders gave in, rather than go through the negative publicity and legal costs associated with continuing along a more conservative path.

Part of the dramatic rise in prices was directly attributable to the rise in home ownership. From 1993 to 2005, the percentage of Americans who owned homes jumped from approximately 63% to approximately 69.2%. Although that is only a 6% increase, those new homeowners were first time buyers.

In any given year, approximately 9-10% of the population purchases a home, and a little better than a third of those buyers are first time home buyers. When the number of first time home buyers was increased, it created a huge demand for first time homes, which drove the prices up. Those home sellers then relocated into "move-up" homes, creating a significant demand for those. Home owners who planned to never move again reconsidered. A home owner living in a moderate home and never expecting to afford a "dream home" now found that "dream home" within range. The increasing prices of moderate housing, combined with historically low interest rates created an opportunity to move to a luxury property that many people never expected to achieve.

Ultimately, the combination of easy credit, low interest rates, high affordability, low unemployment and high immigration all coalesced to create one of the highest periods of home appreciation in history. Like all good things, this too must end.

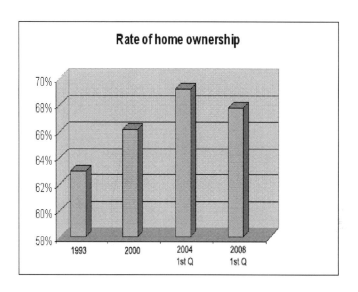

In September of 2003, Treasury Secretary John Snow went before Congress to propose a regulatory agency to oversee Fannie Mae and Freddie Mac, because the White House was concerned about their lending policies. Fannie Mae donated large sums of money to key congress people and no oversight was established. Congressman Barney Frank replied "Fannie Mae and Freddie Mac are not in a crisis". He actually pushed back that Fannie and Freddie needed to do even more to increase home ownership in America.

Hearings occurred in 2004 and 2005. A second attempt to regulate Fannie Mae and Freddie Mac was also blocked. In hearings, Congresswoman Maxine Waters stated that she was unhappy they were trying to "fix something that frankly wasn't broke. Mr. Chairman, we do not have a crisis at Freddie Mac and particular at Fannie Mae".

I submit that if these programs had not allowed unqualified home buyers to purchase homes, the housing recession would not have been nearly as severe. Foreclosures would not be reaching their current levels, and it is unlikely that housing prices would have dipped as low as they have.

Was Lending Money to Everyone Good or Bad?

In the mid 1990's, our firm, Century 21 Keim Realtors, began receiving mortgage company offers that appeared too good to be true. At the time, mortgages were just beginning to appear that offered low down payments and the acceptability of buyers with very low credit scores. These loans came at the price of a high interest rate. If the lender was going to take the risk of loaning to a borrower with limited qualifications, the borrower would have to pay a premium for the money. Later programs allowed nearly anyone to take advantage of low interest loans.

Several of our clients took advantage of these programs and eventually, after paying on the loan for a year or two and establishing a payment history, refinanced them to lower rates. As lenders started reducing restrictions and offering great loan products to buyers, we used those products instead.

In the late 1990's, I received a call from a reporter who wanted me to give him a quote before he fried me in the press. I calmly asked what the problem was, and he replied that our firm had intentionally injured a client by allowing them to take a higher-than-normal interest rate loan. That couple and their children were being thrown out into the street because we had allowed "predatory lenders" to take advantage of the couple.

The interest rate they had paid was 3% over the prevailing rate at that time. I explained to the reporter that the buyer had poor credit and no down payment. The facts were that the buyer was getting into a home with virtually no money out of pocket and a payment of less than $650 per month. To rent a home, like the one they purchased, would be likely to cost $750 per month or more. They were actually able to own a home cheaper than rent.

They were paying a premium in order to try to earn a piece of the American dream. Too many people in the country now expect everything to be given to them. The lender's premium on the mortgage rate was simply a function of the risk the lender was taking in even writing the loan for this borrower. I again stressed that despite the rate, the buyer had actually purchased the home for less per month than they would have paid in rent. It also tuned out that the buyer wasn't able to pay the mortgage because the buyer had gone to prison on charges of armed robbery, not because the payment was too high.

 The reporter was shocked that there actually was another side to the story and that it couldn't easily be spun as mortgage company greed. The reporter found another story and ran that one instead.

 Giving buyers the chance at home ownership is an admirable thing, but it has to be done with sensible rules that won't destroy our country and our way of life. Forcing the banking system to give away money to anyone and then propping it up with government backing by raising taxes is not the answer.

 Please don't misunderstand me. There is plenty of blame to go around. Mortgage brokers made money in fees by writing loans. Appraisers made money estimating the value of homes for those mortgage brokers. Financial institutions made money packaging the loans and selling them to Fannie Mae or selling them as Mortgage Backed Securities. Even Wall Street Rating Agencies made money by rating the mortgage backed securities. There is plenty of guilt to go around, but it starts with government intervention.

The mortgage system is broken and needs to be fixed by people that are not part of the problem. Congress can't effectively fix the problem, because they are much of the blame for our current economic situation.

Chapter 2:
Understanding the Options

    The primary focus of this book is on educating consumers about the short sale process and educating real estate professionals on the steps required to assist clients through a short sale process. There are situations when a short sale is not a home owner's best course of action, and there are situations where a short sale is absolutely the home owner's best alternative.

    There are two major reasons to consider a "short sale". The first reason is that the home owners are behind in their mortgage payments and their home will be foreclosed if something doesn't happen soon. The second situation is if the home owner needs to sell because of a divorce, job relocation, illness or other issue, and is under water in their mortgage, which means they owe more than the property can be sold for, with closing costs, in the current market.

There are different sets of choices depending on whether the home is going into foreclosure or the home owner is simply being forced to sell. We'll handle them separately.

A Foreclosure Story

Like everyone reading this book, I'm a normal guy, working every day to earn enough to pay my mortgage, my kid's dental bills, the family car, a few credit cards and possibly a nice vacation. The way I earn a living is by operating a real estate firm in Pennsylvania. Our firm, Century 21 Keim, sells homes, farm, land, investment properties and businesses. Writing books and speaking at events is a sideline.

Part of my job is to represent our clients in the purchase and sale of properties. In some cases, those clients are not individuals, but rather banks and other lenders. When banks and mortgage companies foreclose on a home, it's our job to sell that home as quickly as possible. Most of the time, I don't get called until after the bank has possession of the property, although that is not always the case.

Last year, I was asked to meet the Sheriff at a home in Bangor, Pennsylvania, just off Route I-80, and within commuting distance of New York City. The former owner of the home, Charley, stood on the front porch of the home, with a large dog, and waved a gun near his head. He was threatening to kill himself if the Sheriff tried to remove him from the property. The Sheriff called the Pennsylvania State Police and an animal control group.

I walked close to the porch and spoke with Charley. He was a retired military veteran. His wife had left him and he had become unemployed. His mortgage was a Veteran's Administration Loan and, obviously, he had fallen behind on payments. The lender foreclosed on the home, but had failed to properly evict him from the property. I really felt his pain. Unfortunately, there was nothing I could do for him at this point. It was too late to salvage anything for him.

As it turned out, Charley's gun was unloaded and wouldn't have fired even if it were loaded. He was taken into custody to receive psychological treatments. The questions in my mind were "How do people get to this point?" and "How can we help people before this happens?"

People in Tough Situations

If you're watching the news, I'm certain you're seeing the huge number of people being laid off by firms across the country. Contrary to popular belief, these companies aren't trying to hurt their workers. They're trying to survive without filing bankruptcy and without losing everything they have, just like you, me and everyone we know.

Across the country, there are people in pain. People are losing their homes because of job loss, divorce, a death in the family, a prolonged illness, incarceration or any number of other reasons. Home owners call me after they've fallen so far behind in their mortgage payments, they can't see daylight anymore. Part of my job is to find a way to either keep them in their homes, or to get the home sold with a minimal amount of damage to their credit.

The familiar situation starts like this. John and Sally purchased a home for $150,000 in 2006. They borrowed $140,000 against the home, and then used a Lowes Credit Card to buy $6500 in materials to improve the home. They got the home into the perfect condition and were paying all bills on time until Sally was laid off from her job.

The family was still able to pay their mortgage, car loan and credit cards as long as John was able to maintain his schedule of overtime, but the health insurance had been through Sally's company and now they'd have to pay a Cobra payment in addition to their normal bills in order to keep their healthcare.

John's company cut back on production as sales of their products slid, and John's overtime was eliminated. After two weeks, his hours were cut back as well. The family's income was no longer high enough to pay all the bills. John and Sally continued paying the mortgage on time, but let the credit card bills, cable bill and car loans slip. In fact, they borrowed more on a Citibank card in order to pay the Cobra payment for the month.

The couple considered selling the home, but the real estate agent they met with explained that prices had declined, and their home was now only worth $135,000, which was less than they owed. Their closing costs to sell the home would be in excess of $8000, which meant they would net less than $127,000 after closing costs, or $13,000 less than they currently owed. They didn't have the $13,000.

John's company finally shut down production and laid off all production workers with the hope that they'd be rehired in ninety days. The couple had exhausted their credit limit on their cards and barely had enough to buy food and pay the electric bill, so they stopped paying the mortgage.

    The mortgage company was relentless with their phone calls, asking when the mortgage would be brought current. After John and Sally missed three payments, the lender sent a demand notice, stating that if the couple didn't bring the mortgage current within thirty days, the bank would be forced to foreclose on the home. Worse, the couple now owed three payments, late fees, and a lot of legal fees that were listed on the demand notice.

    Sally made several frantic calls to the mortgage company, trying to extend the mortgage or refinance. She left messages, and was on hold for an hour at a time, trying to get to someone who could help them.

    Suddenly, John and Sally started receiving mail from attorneys claiming they could save the home through bankruptcy, Realtors asking if they'd like to sell the property prior to a judicial sale, and other experts selling their services. At the end of the week, they received a call from someone who claimed to be able to help them stay in their home. All they had to do was sign their home over to this investment group, and the group would allow them to stay in the home and simply pay a rental fee back to the investment group. They sounded sincere, but Sally didn't know.

This situation is not uncommon. It is being repeated tens of thousands of times across the country. In order to deal with this situation, whether you are a home owner in trouble, or whether you are a Realtor trying to guide a home owner through these challenges, you need to know your options.

The Options when facing Foreclosure

Merriam-Webster's online dictionary defines foreclosure as "*a legal proceeding that bars or extinguishes a mortgagor's right of redeeming a mortgaged estate.*" Foreclosure is a legal process by which a mortgage company, bank or other lender takes possession of a property. A foreclosure is performed in order to satisfy a mortgage on the property that is not performing. In other words, if you're not making the payments on the mortgage, the only recourse a lender has is to take back the house using this legal process of foreclosure.

The two primary forms of foreclosure in the United States are judicial sale and foreclosure by power of sale. A third form of foreclosure, known as strict foreclosure, is used only in New Hampshire and Vermont. In order to understand you or your client's rights and obligations, you'll have to determine which form of foreclosure is utilized in your state. Our discussion of the foreclosure process is a broad one because each state has its own specific rules, regulations and systems.

Foreclosure by Judicial Sale

In essence, Foreclosure by Judicial Sale is simply a foreclosure through the court system. This form of foreclosure is a legal action and requires all parties to be notified prior to the sale in order for the foreclosing lender to acquire valid title to the property. All parties who have claim to the property, including equity lien holders, second mortgages or any other lien holders, must be notified prior to the sale.

Although each state performs judicial sales differently, in order to foreclose by judicial sale, the lender must file a suit against the home owner for the failure of the home owner to follow the terms of the mortgage. The home owner is notified of the impending sale and is given the opportunity to pay the mortgage up to date.

If the home owner is unable to bring the loan current, a court appointed official, such as a Sheriff, conducts the sale. In a Judicial Sale, any proceeds at the sale of the property are paid first to the first lien holder or first mortgage, next to any subsequent liens in order of their position against the property, and finally the borrower if any money remains from the sale.

If the sale proceeds are not enough to satisfy the mortgage, the lender may file a judgment against the borrower for the difference. This is known as a deficiency judgment. If the mortgage was $200,000 and the sale produced only $150,000, the lender may file a judgment for the $50,000 difference. However, in some parts of the country, the deficiency judgment may be reduced by "fair value" legislation. "Fair value" deficiencies are based on the difference between the "fair value" of the property and the sale price, which benefits borrowers in declining markets.

Foreclosure by Power of Sale

In states that allow foreclosure by Power of Sale, the foreclosing lender has the ability to sell the property without the supervision of the court system. This is often a more rapid foreclosure process. In some states, the foreclosure is subject to a judicial review after the foreclosure sale.

In some areas, the foreclosure by power of sale is facilitated by a third party, known as a trustee, who holds a deed of trust to the property. The benefit to having a trustee handle the sale is that the lender may bid on the property at the sale and buy the property back.

Owner's Right of Redemption

Known as statutory redemption, some states allow a borrower to redeem the mortgage, affectively buying back the property, for a period after the foreclosure sale. The term of this redemption period varies from state to state but is typically between six months and a year. Again, this redemption is not available in all states and you must consult an expert to determine your specific rights in your area.

The Seven Options to Avoid Foreclosure

Despite what you may have heard from other sources, lenders do not want to foreclose on your home. Banks, mortgage companies and mortgage servicers are in business to lend money and make a return, called interest, on the money they've lent, called principal. When a home is foreclosed by the bank, the bank usually loses.

A lender may spend thousands of dollars on the legal process of foreclosing on a home, and still be limited by the value of the home in the current real estate market. Worse, a lender can potentially receive the home in damaged condition. Some homeowners who are facing foreclosure remove everything from the home, including appliances, light fixtures and in some cases, kitchen cabinets, toilets and sinks! Some homeowners in foreclosure, frustrated by the idea of losing their home, physically destroy it.

In states where statutory redemption is common, the prior home owner may be able to remain in the home for six months to a year after the foreclosure sale. This costs the lender even more money in lost payments.

If you or your client is in risk of foreclosure or in the foreclosure process, you'll need to move quickly to either sell the home or negotiate terms. If the owner plans to keep the home, often the faster the negotiation begins, the better the end result for the owner. Missed payments are added onto the balance owed on the home. Late fees, attorney's fees, and other court costs can continue to erode any chance the owner has of receiving money for the home or negotiating a settlement.

There are seven possible options for home owners facing the specter of foreclosure. If you are a Realtor, you should be offering all alternatives to your clients so they understand their rights. If you are a home owner, you should realize that some of these options are highly preferable to foreclosure or a short sale, but they may not work in your situation. They include:

1. Mortgage Modification
2. Repayment Plan
3. Forbearance Agreement
4. Re-instatement of Mortgage
5. Short Sale
6. The Deed in Lieu of Foreclosure
7. Bankruptcy

Mortgage Modification

Many borrowers are trapped because they financed their homes using Adjustable Rate Mortgages (ARMs) that were based on one of several indexes that are rising. Many of these borrowers qualified at the low introductory rate. Some borrowers didn't understand that the rate could increase, and other borrowers believed they could afford the increases if they occurred. Other situations can lead to the borrower falling behind in their payments. They may have had a serious illness, job loss or death in the family.

Worse, in some cases of subprime loans, property taxes were not escrowed, which creates a situation where a home owner is hit once or twice a year with a very large bill in addition to the mortgage.

A mortgage modification or loan modification occurs when a lender agrees to allow the home owner to modify the terms of the original mortgage. As stated earlier in this text, the lender doesn't want to foreclose on the home, but the lender also wants to insure payment.

The Federal Government is pressuring lenders to renegotiate the terms of loans if the borrower is unable to repay the loan based on the current terms. In some cases, the lender is willing to reduce the interest rate to a fixed rate. Beware that some of these fixed rates may create "negative amortization", which means the amount the borrower is paying may not cover the entire amount owed, and additional principal is then tacked on the end of the mortgage. In these cases, the loan is extended to a longer term.

Although rare at this time, another renegotiated term includes reducing the principal balance to reflect the current property value in order to avoid foreclosure.

Forbearance Agreement

A forbearance agreement is an agreement from the bank or the mortgage company to allow a borrower to delay making mortgage payments for a short period of time. As with many of these negotiations, lenders are more willing to discuss options if the borrower had a significant reason for their failure to pay and now has the ability to begin paying. These issues can include a serious illness, job loss or death in the family.

In order for a forbearance agreement to be accepted by the lender, the borrower must contact the lender as quickly as possible. Once the home goes into the foreclosure process, late payments, legal fees and other costs are added to the balance on the mortgage.

Forbearance agreements are most often found in small local banks and credit unions, although some large lenders have negotiated these terms during the 2007-2009 recession.

Repayment Plan

If a borrower falls behind on their mortgage, the lender may be willing to modify the payment schedule in order for the home owner to catch up on their loan, creating a new repayment plan. This modification process happens most often when a borrower had a really strong reason for their missed loan payments. If the borrower had a serious illness, job loss or death in the family, the lender may be more willing to negotiate different loan terms.

The lender is unlikely to accept a repayment plan unless there is strong evidence that the borrower can now make those payments. An example might be a person who lost a job but now had another, or a person who was ill and has now recovered and can show proof they are again earning enough to satisfy the mortgage payments.

A new payment plan is created between the lender and the borrower. The lender may add the missed payments to the end of the loan, or the lender may require additional payments or larger payments until the borrower is paid up to date.

Unlike a mortgage modification, the rate and terms of the loan are typically not altered, and unlike a forbearance agreement, the borrower is typically required to begin making payments immediately in order to show good faith and begin catching up on their loan.

Re-instatement of Mortgage

In any state in the country, the borrower has the right to catch up the mortgage prior to the judicial sale, sheriff sale or sale through the power of sale process. In order to avoid foreclosure, the borrower must typically pay the outstanding missed payments, any late fees, attorney's costs and other fees prior to the sale. Check with an attorney to see your rights and obligations in your particular state. This is called a re-instatement of the mortgage.

In some cases, the lender may temporarily stall the judicial sale if the borrower has a good case that the lender will benefit from the stall. For example, if the borrower has an agreement to purchase the home from a qualified buyer, but is unable to settle the property prior to the sale, the lender may postpone the date. Additionally, if the borrower has significant proof that he or she will be able to pay the outstanding balance and fees with a tax refund, disability or estate settlement or some other lump sum that is pending, the lender may prolong the sale date.

Short Sale

The majority of this book is dedicated to the short sale process because there are several benefits to both the lender and the home owner. Asking a lender for a short sale is simply asking the lender to take less than you owe on the property as payment for the property. This is far preferable to walking away and having a foreclosure or bankruptcy on your credit report.

Deed in Lieu of Foreclosure

A deed in lieu of foreclosure is simply your agreement to voluntarily deed your property back to the bank or mortgage company. Many Realtors and attorneys call these "friendly foreclosures" because, in essence, you are losing your property or home to the bank. However, you may not damage your credit as significantly as you would with an involuntary foreclosure. This is typically a last resort plan.

Bankruptcy

Five of the six prior methods of avoiding foreclosure are at the discretion of the bank or mortgage company that holds the mortgage against a property. The lender simply doesn't have to agree to any of them, with the exception of re-instatement where the borrower pays the outstanding balance. The lender can make a decision that they'd prefer to continue with a foreclosure on the property. This happens when the lender believes there may be value in the property after foreclosure above what you are offering, or when the negotiator representing the lender feels it is in their best interest to pass the property off to foreclosure rather than negotiate.

If all else fails, the borrower can still stall the process by filing bankruptcy. Bankruptcy will halt the foreclosure process and could possibly force the lender to negotiate with the borrower.

If you or your client plan to keep the home, bankruptcy may be a solid method of stalling the foreclosure process long enough to turn around your or your client's financial situation.

If you or your client is planning to sell the home, and simply need time to get the property sold, there are several reasons I would avoid the bankruptcy process. First, it creates another level the owner and Realtor have to deal with in order to get an approval on the sale of a property. The court has to approve a sale and may open negotiations to include payments to creditors who do not currently have any lien against the property.

Second, the additional time necessary to get an approval from a bankruptcy court may scare away potential buyers of the property. Last, bankruptcy affects your credit score for a very long time. Lawyers and lenders tell our clients that they may be able to purchase a car or home within a couple years of filing a bankruptcy. However, in the current state of credit scoring, that bankruptcy will remain on your credit report for seven to ten years, causing you questions and curbing your ability to raise your credit score for a significant period of time. Although you may not think you'll ever own a home again, do you really know where you'll be in six or seven years? Will you be in a different place in your life?

Why bother avoiding foreclosure?

One of the common questions I'm asked when discussing options with a client is why they should take the time and effort to try to avoid a foreclosure. After all, their credit is already shot. They've missed three mortgage payments, two car payments and sixteen credit card bills. Their employment is shaky, at best, and they don't believe they'll ever have good credit again.

At the point when you only have late payments, your credit is correctible. After selling your home or renegotiating your debt, you can begin the process of paying bills on time and rebuilding your credit. Late payments don't look good, but they are a far cry from foreclosure or bankruptcy.

Consider this situation. You may not ever purchase a home again, but at some point you may need a car loan. That foreclosure or bankruptcy will stay on your credit for seven to ten years, affecting you a long time into the future. Your credit score will affect the interest rate you pay for credit cards, and any other long term payment plans you attempt to set up. Consider the problem of trying to co-sign for your son or daughter's student loans in four or five years. It may not seem like a problem today, but it could be a huge problem in a few years.

Another issue is that your credit will even affect where you live. We've had dozens of clients with foreclosures and bankruptcies apply to rent homes. The property owner's first question to us is "If they couldn't afford a mortgage, how are they going to afford to pay my rent? They had something invested in their home and they lost it. They have nothing invested in my rental property." You may ultimately be turned down by many landlords because of the credit issues.

The Risk of Waiting Too Long

Timing is critical when you're trying to avoid a foreclosure. Too many of my clients call me when it's very late in the foreclosure process. The more quickly a home owner can get to experts, the better. If you need to sell your home prior to a Sheriff sale or a judicial sale, you need to have time to find a buyer, secure financing and close on the home. While it is possible the lender will extend the judicial sale, it is never a guarantee.

As an example, one of our clients this year called less than 60 days before the Sheriff sale and asked if we could get the home sold. Looking at the property, the owner had some equity, so we were certain we could get her out without attempting a short sale. The home had a value of about $245,000 and the owner owed $175,000.

She suggested we list the property at $259,900 and test the market. I explained that we certainly could not "test the market", because she would surely end up losing everything. The current average time a home is on the market in this particular marketplace was 78 days. Worse, the average time a buyer requires to close is between 30 and 45 days. That means we need 108 to 123 days to get a normal market price.

Based on having fewer than 60 days, and the time to close being 30 to 45, we had only 2 to 4 weeks to actually secure a buyer, in a slowing real estate market. In a situation where time is so critical, the home needs to be priced below market price in order to attract more buyers and secure offers. The owner was unhappy with our suggestion, but the reality is that if we tried a high price for 2 weeks unsuccessfully, we'd be left trying to sell the home in just days.

In many markets around the country, the average time to sell a home is in excess of six months to a year. When timing is critical, the owner must work with the Realtor to determine what price will attract the few buyers in the marketplace. If that price doesn't work, then they have to determine what price will be sufficient to attract investors to make offers.

The Four Options in a "Need to Move" Situation

Assuming that you wouldn't be reading this section if you or your client doesn't owe more than the property can be sold for in the current marketplace, we'll eliminate the obvious choice of selling your home for more than you owe plus closing costs. The remaining options include:

1. Rent the home
2. Deed in Lieu of Foreclosure
3. Pay the difference between the current value and what you owe
4. Short Sale

Renting the Home

Renting the home in order to cover the mortgage until the market turns and prices rise is always a possibility. If you are the owner of the property, be prepared to hold onto the home for a period of time. The real estate market may take a period of time to recover. It is often not a quick process. Even once the market starts moving in a positive direction, there is a significant time lag between when the housing market picks up and when prices begin again to rise.

Real estate is a commodity like any other commodity. Prices are a function of supply and demand. If there is a heavy supply of homes in your marketplace and a light demand, prices may fall or they may stay stable, but they will not rise. Demand, or many buyers chasing that one house, is what causes prices to rise. Too many home owners believe they "charge" for a house, but the reality is that price is based on what buyers are willing to pay to own a property like yours. They determine this value by comparing your home with others for sale.

Putting it simply, in many parts of the country you may not see those high 2006 prices for five to ten years. The excess inventory of homes in the market has to be reabsorbed before prices can rise. That is simple economics.

If you still choose to rent your home, there are several challenges that you should be aware of. First, you will likely have periods of vacancy when a tenant moves out and another hasn't yet moved in. You should be prepared to handle that loss. Second, tenants may not take care of your home the same way you do. Have you ever rented a car, and spilled something in it? Oh, well, it's a rental. That may be the same view of your tenants.

There are also potential tax consequences of keeping the property as a rental for a significant period of time. The property makes a shift from being a "personal residence" to being an investment property. When you sell the property, you could be subject to Capital Gains taxes for having an investment.

On the other hand, real estate makes a great investment over time. The tenants pay down your mortgage, and eventually the value rises. What you'll have to decide is whether or not you're cut out to be a landlord. You should also investigate all the legal and tax implications before you move forward with this decision.

Deed in Lieu of Foreclosure

As stated in the prior section, a deed in lieu of foreclosure is simply your agreement to voluntarily deed your property back to the bank or mortgage company. This is not the best avenue for borrowers in most situations, although it can be a way out. The borrower is still losing their home to the lender, but the borrower may not damage his or her credit as significantly as he or she would with an involuntary foreclosure. As mentioned in the prior section, this is typically a last resort plan.

Short Sale

As stated in the last section, the majority of this book is dedicated to the short sale process because there are several benefits to both the lender and the home owner. Asking a lender for a short sale is simply asking the lender to take less than you owe on the property as payment for the property. This is far preferable to walking away and having a foreclosure or bankruptcy on your credit report.

Summary

Whether you're a home owner that is underwater in your mortgage, or a Realtor attempting to advise clients, you need to understand all the options that are available. If the property is in foreclosure or going into foreclosure, there are possible ways to negotiate modifications to a loan in order to remain in the home. Those include mortgage modification, forbearance, and setting up a new payment plan or schedule. If the mortgage company is unwilling to negotiation, the home owner may simply give up and deed the home back to the lender through the process of deed in lieu of foreclosure, or the owner may file bankruptcy to stay in the home. If the home owner would prefer to move, a short sale might be a solid alternative.

If the property is not in foreclosure, but the owner is upside down in their mortgage and needs to move due to a divorce, job relocation or other reason, then options include renting the home, giving the home back to the bank or negotiating a short sale.

In any of these cases, it pays to seek advice of a skilled professional.

Chapter 3:
The Risks and Rewards of Short Sales

Selling your home through a short sale is not for everyone. There are pros and cons, or benefits and challenges to the process. Before you do anything, you should consider all the possible options available, which are outlined in the last section, and perhaps consult an accountant, Realtor and even an attorney.

Pros of short sale

What are the benefits or positive aspects of agreeing to sell a home with a short sale? Why even consider a short sale? Isn't it far easier to stop the harassing phone calls from the lender by simply walking away from the home, or giving the home back to the lender in a deed in lieu?

When a lender forecloses on a property or takes back the property through a deed in lieu, they still retain the right to go after the home owner for the difference between the amount that the lender sold the home for and the amount that was owed on the home. This is known as a deficiency judgment. What this means is that the lender may continue to hound you forever until the debt is repaid or you file bankruptcy.

> *Quick Reference Guide of Short Sale Pros*
>
> *Avoid Foreclosure*
> *Avoid Bankruptcy*
> *Avoid Deficiency Judgment*
> *Lender Paid Closing Costs*
> *Potentially Better Credit at the End.*

To clarify, there are laws and regulations in different parts of the country that limit or disallow this practice. There are also laws being considered that may reduce or impact this practice. Since this book is being written in a snapshot in time, and the mortgage crisis is fluidly changing, you must consult a professional. You should always determine your rights and obligations prior to making a decision, and legal counsel is the best method to understand these.

Another strong benefit is the possibility of preserving some credit for the borrower. Although we don't have access to the formulas used by credit agencies to determine an individual's credit score, we can guestimate the potential outcome based on our work with customers in short sale situations. Unfortunately, the credit reporting agencies appear to do a better job hiding their formulas than the government hides their secrets.

Our analysis suggests that while a foreclosure may cost the borrower 200 to 300 points of credit score, a short sale may only cost 80 points to 120 points. Again, you can't take these numbers to be gospel, but it does appear that a short sale impacts your credit significantly less than a foreclosure or bankruptcy, meaning that you can rebuild your credit more quickly.

One further benefit of the short sale process is that the lender typically pays the bills for the borrower's closing costs to sell the property. In essence, these costs are deducted from the net that the lender receives at settlement, but they are not paid by the borrower.

Cons of short sale

Several aspects of a short sale concern home sellers, and many that concern potential buyers of homes sold subject to a short sale. For example, the home owner may go through a lot of work and pain to locate a buyer, negotiate a sale, and fill out all the required documentation of the lender just to be turned down by the lender. Although we've found this situation to be rare because the lender is more likely to respond with a counter proposal, it is still a risk.

The reward of avoiding a bankruptcy or foreclosure on the owner's credit is often worth the risk of a denial.

The risk for buyers in this scenario is that they could potentially waste sixty or ninety days waiting for an approval on the purchase of a home only to be shot down by the lender. In many cases, however, the risk is worth the wait. The potential value the buyer may receive in purchasing the home at a discount may be worth the risk of being denied.

> ## Quick Reference Guide of Short Sale Cons
>
> Lender May Say "No"
>
> Owner Receives No Proceeds
>
> Possible Personal Note for Deficiency
>
> Long Time for Answers

Another common complaint by home owners considering short sales is that the owner may not receive proceeds from the sale of the home. "We need money in order to move!" Unfortunately, the home owner made a commitment to purchase the home, take out the mortgage and made a guarantee to pay that loan back. In a short sale, we are asking the lender to take less than they are owed. In some cases, we are asking the lender to take far less than they are owed. They gave the home owner a loan in the first place, and they are taking a significant loss. They are certainly not going to give money back to the borrower. They'll simply foreclose and resell the home at a later time.

Worse than the home owner receiving no proceeds from the sale is when the bank or lender only agrees to accept the short sale if the borrower agrees to take a personal loan for part of the loss. Although this means the borrower may have to make an additional payment on a home they no longer own, it also significantly reduces their liability on the property and again, can save the borrower's credit from the damage and stigma of a bankruptcy or foreclosure.

Additionally, the borrower doesn't have to accept the lender's proposal either. The borrower can decide, after receiving this proposal, to file bankruptcy or walk away and allow a foreclosure. Typically, if the lender is requiring a personal note or loan for part of the balance, it is because the borrower has sufficient income to justify the expense and, in our experience, the loan is typically for only part of the shortfall. The lender is trying to share the pain.

Chapter 4:
The Short Sale – Step by Step

Regardless of whether you are a home owner attempting to get out from under a crushing mortgage payment, or a Realtor attempting to assist that home owner, you'll need to understand all the steps necessary to get a short sale accomplished. The short sale process can be long and complicated. This chapter will focus on the typical steps required by most lenders to facilitate a short sale, with some information included for specific lender practices. The length of time to obtain an approval on a short sale request has risen significantly over the past twelve months. Some lenders are actively telling us that they need ninety days to review a short sale request.

One of the challenges of putting a short sale together, whether you are a property owner or a Realtor, is that many buyers are unwilling to wait sixty or ninety days to find out whether or not they've been able to purchase a home. There are many properties on the market for sale for a buyer to choose from without having to wait, so we have to entice a buyer to hang in on the transaction.

An additional complication occurs when the home owner has more than one mortgage against the property. There may be a second mortgage that the home owner took out at the time of purchase, or there may be a home equity loan or line of credit the owner used to make some improvement, or any other lien against the property. We'll begin by first explaining the short sale process with a lender, and then expand to include second mortgages later in this chapter.

Requesting a short sale, in a nut shell, is finding a buyer, negotiating an offer on the home, contacting the lender, obtaining all the documents the lender requires for approval, and then staying in contact with the lender until they approve, deny or counter your proposal.

Again, as I have stressed throughout this book, have an expert assist you with this process. Seek the advice of an attorney, Realtor, accountant and any other professional you might require to insure the process is done correctly, and to insure you're making the appropriate decision for your situation.

Step 1: Contact Your Lender for Information

Most lenders will not approve a short sale until there is an actual offer to negotiate. Banks and mortgage services are typically understaffed and very busy trying to work out situations with other clients who already have offers on their properties. They don't have the time and resources to analyze every possibility.

However, since short sale approvals are taking considerable periods of time, it makes sense to find out who you need to speak with and what the lender requires the owner or Realtor to supply. In most cases, the lender has a "short sale" package that includes a list of all the forms the lender requires.

My suggestion to either a Realtor or a home owner is to contact your lender immediately and let them know you are working on securing a buyer and need a copy of their short sale package. If you are the home owner, be prepared to sit on the phone for a half hour to two hours in order to obtain the information. You will be passed around from department to department. If you are a Realtor, make sure you get a signed letter from the home owner allowing you to discuss the owner's finances with the lender. A sample letter will be included in the next chapter. This letter must include the loan number, borrower's full names, social security numbers for the borrowers and the address of the property.

You will contact the bank using the phone number on your mortgage statement, or you can get a list of direct numbers from our website at www.RealEstatesNextLevel.com. Since phone numbers are constantly changing for lenders, I believe that keeping a regularly updated list on the web is better than simply printing the list in this text. You, or your Realtor, should contact the workout department at the lender.

Once you have the appropriate person on the phone, attempt to get a direct phone number to the department, a fax number and an email address. It is imperative you get a direct phone number so you won't have to go through the same process of calling your lender's toll free number and being transferred back and forth across the world for an hour. The fax number and email address are helpful because you will find that, although you will get better results actually speaking with a representative, there are times you will get a better response by emailing or faxing.

The last part of this step is to ask for a list of all the documentation and forms necessary to apply for a short sale once an offer is received. If the lender tells you to call back when you have an offer, let them know that you may be close with a buyer and want to start the process. Getting the information will save time later.

Step 2: Market Your Property and Find a Buyer

Marketing a property that requires a short sale may also be a challenge for several reasons. First, you must notify any potential buyers that any offer must be approved by your lender. This will scare some buyers away from your home because they don't want to wait for someone else to approve the sale. This will attract some investors who believe

they can "steal" the home, because they've seen on late night television that banks will accept almost any offer. This is simply not true.

The components of marketing any property successfully include pricing, staging and marketing. Staging is simply presenting your property in the best possible light in order to attract buyers to offer on your property rather than competing properties. Pricing entails carefully selecting the correct asking price in order to attract potential buyers. There are methods to selecting correct price positions based on recent sales and competing properties for sale.[iv]

Marketing can encompass web marketing, multiple listing marketing, print media marketing and many other forms. When attempting to sell your home for top dollar, I recommend picking up a copy of my best selling book "How to Sell Your Home in Any Market" from Sphinx Legal Publishing. It is available on Amazon, Barnes and Noble, Borders, Target and many other places.

Step 3: Negotiating an Agreement

The typical home requiring a short sale sells for a bit less than other properties. The primary reason for this anomaly is that the buyer must have a reason to go through the pain of purchasing a home through a short sale. Historically, short sale properties sold to investors because they were the few with the fortitude to wait weeks to months to find out whether or not the sale would actually go through.

Imagine the stress of moving to a new home and perhaps a new school district. Consider the stress on your family. Now add to that stress the idea that unlike most real estate transactions, where a buyer knows within a day or two whether or not the owner will accept the offer, the buyer may have to wait several months for an answer. Worse, if the lender accepts the buyers offer, the buyer needs to be prepared to settle and move quickly.

Most buyers who are selling another home need to plan their move very carefully. They can't rely on the hope that this transaction will settle. They need to be out of their home by a certain date and need a place to move. If they have a sixty day window to move from their home and they won't find out a response about the short sale from the lender for forty-five days, that gives them little or no time to find another home should this transaction fall through.

Because short sale transactions are typically limited to investors and those who do not "have" to move by a certain date, the pool of potential buyers is smaller than for that of other homes. Enticing buyers to purchase a short sale home over one that doesn't have the same challenges often requires some consideration in price.

If you're an owner is this situation, you may be offended at selling your property slightly below market, but please consider that the lender won't allow you to receive any proceeds anyway, so you're not taking that direct loss.

An added complication is that many of the owners of homes requiring a short sale are in default on their mortgage or at risk of default. That means that the owner may have to get the home sold more quickly than the typical home in the area. If the Sheriff is locking the doors and auctioning the home in ninety days and the typical market time in a slow market in your area is six months, you need to be priced below the market in order to attract buyers to your property first.

Arm's Length Transactions

It is also important to note that many home owners have attempted to sell their home through the process of a short sale to relatives or business associates. Most lenders are now requiring an affidavit to be signed that the sale is an "arm's length" transaction, meaning the buyer is not a blood relative, or directly connected to you. The lender will not accept a loss while the home owner is benefiting in some way from that loss.

Risk of Selling with a Short Sale: Full Disclosure

When a home owner negotiates the sale of a property with a buyer, the home owner is promising to deliver the property to the buyer in return for consideration, or a certain sales price. If the home owner cannot deliver the property because they are unable to pay off the debt against the property, they may be considered in default and they may be subject to legal action against them.

A Realtor must do their best to protect a home owner from making the mistake of offering a property or negotiating a sale without properly disclosing the challengers and potential risks of purchasing the property when it is subject to a short sale.

There are four primary components of minimizing the home owner's risk of legal action from the home buyers or other parties associated with the transaction. First, have an attorney review any documentation. Second, clearly explain the short sale process to the buyer. Third, provide the buyer with a strong disclosure statement describing the home owner's situation. Finally, be certain the sales contract contains language explaining that the home sale is contingent upon a short sale and that the agreement will be null and void if the lender refuses to accept the short sale proposal, and that the seller has no responsibility to reimburse the buyer for any fees, charges or expenses incurred through the purchasing process. In essence, when in doubt, disclose disclose disclose. Home sellers must protect themselves from further legal action by disclosing.

The first sample form, included on the next page, is a sample disclosure for a home seller to provide a home buyer. The seller, or seller's Realtor, should have the buyer sign a form like this in order to expressly disclose the possibility that the sale may not close due to a rejection by the lender. This form, like all forms in this book, is a sample and should be reviewed by an attorney in the home owner's state to meet any applicable laws and requirements.

Seller's Disclosure to Buyers

Owners: _____
Property Address: _____

Property seller discloses and Buyer acknowledges that the property seller's proceeds on the sale of the property may be less than the amount necessary to pay off outstanding liens secured by the property.

Liens against the property may include, but are not limited to, mortgages, home equity loans, lines of credit, tax claims, unemployment compensation claims, home owners' association fees, condominium fees and legal judgments.

Any sales contract shall be conditioned upon all holders of any outstanding liens releasing the property from the liens at time of settlement. This release may require the lien holders to accept a payoff of less than the full amount due to that lien holder.

Should property seller be unable to transfer the property free and clear of liens and encumbrances at time of settlement, buyer shall not hold property seller responsible for any losses incurred in the buyer's attempt to secure, inspect or finance the property.

Sellers: _____
         _____

Buyers: _____
        _____

Addendum to Sale's Contract

As with the seller's disclosure to buyers, the seller or seller's Realtor or attorney should attach an addendum to the sales contract explicitly making the contract subject to approval by the bank, mortgage company or lien holders. An example of such a form follows:

Short Sale Addendum to Sale's Contract (example)

Sellers: _____
Buyers: _____
Property Address: _____
Date of Sale's Contract: _____

1. Property seller discloses and Buyer acknowledges that the property seller's proceeds on the sale of the property may be less than the amount necessary to pay off outstanding liens secured by the property. This process is known as a short sale.

2. Liens against the property may include, but are not limited to, mortgages, home equity loans, lines of credit, tax claims, unemployment compensation claims, home owners' association fees, condominium fees and legal judgments.

3. The sale's contract for the property is contingent upon the seller obtaining approval of the terms and conditions of the sale's contract by all lenders and lien

holders that are requested to accept a final payment of less than the full balance due on the mortgage or lien.

4. Seller makes no representations regarding the length of time necessary for all lenders and lien holders to respond to the sale's contract. Buyer acknowledges that the lenders and lien holders may take an extended period to respond.

5. If lenders or lien holders require a change in the terms or conditions of the sale's contract as a condition of approval for the contract, seller will communicate these changes to the buyer in writing within 72 hours of receipt. Buyer shall either accept or refuse any of these changes to the contract within 72 hours of their receipt. If buyer accepts the changes, the contract will be changed by addendum to include the changes. If the buyer declines the changes, the sale's contract shall be declared null and void and all deposit monies shall be returned to buyer.

6. All other terms and conditions of the sale's contract shall stay in full effect.

7. Buyer and seller are advised to seek professional legal and financial advice before making a final sale's contract on a property requiring a short sale.

Sellers: _____
         _____
Buyers: _____
         _____

Step 4: Put Together a Short Sale Package for your Lender

Hopefully, by the time you receive an offer on your property, you'll already have the full short sale package and you'll have started filling it out. It is imperative to get this package to the lender as quickly as possible and then to follow up with the lender to make sure they received it and that they are processing it.

Whether you are the home owner, negotiating with the lender directly, or a Realtor or attorney attempting to work on behalf of the home owner, there is a lot of information that needs to be provided to the lender. Some of the information will have to be filled out by the home owner, because it directly involves the home owner's financial situation. Some of the forms are better prepared by a Realtor, title insurance agent or attorney.

Although every lender is slightly different, the typical documents required in a short sale package include:

1. A Cover Letter
2. An authorization for the Realtor or attorney to speak with the lender
3. Seller's Hardship Letter
4. Hardship Documentation - Copies of documentation related to owner's hardship
5. Seller's Financial Statement or Income, Expense and Asset Worksheet
6. W-2 forms for past two years
7. Two months pay stubs

8. Two to three months bank statements
9. Repair estimate for any necessary repairs to property
10. Agreement of Sale or Contract to purchase the property
11. Realtor's competitive market analysis
12. Photos of the home (interior and exterior)
13. Seller Net Sheet
14. Payoff statements from any other lenders or liens against the property
15. Preliminary HUD 1 settlement sheet

Other forms that the lender may ask for include:

1. Title search of the property
2. Special forms

Each of these forms or requirements will be explained in detail over the next several pages.

Cover Letter

A cover letter should be concise, explaining exactly what you wish to do and how you wish to do it. The letter should include the full names of all owners of the property, the mortgage account number, the owner's contact information and the owner's social security numbers. The letter should specifically state that you are requesting a short sale and what amount you are requesting the lender to take. A sample letter is below.

Dear Mr. Bigmoneylender,

    The loan on my home at 2625 Happy Hollow in Wildwood, NJ is delinquent and I am unable to keep making mortgage payments. I have an offer to purchase my home, which is included with this package, and I would like to request your bank accept a short payoff.

    My Realtor has estimated the bank would net $203,537 with this transaction. My current mortgage balance is approximately $232,500.

    My loan number is 83-2098712 and my social security number is 000-00-0000.

    I have included, with this package, all the documentation you requested to consider this short sale on my home. Please contact my Realtor, Susan Potter at 515-000-0000 or me at 515-000-0001 at your earliest convenience so we can determine how to proceed.

    Sincerely,

    Matt Reynolds

Realtor or Attorney's Authorization

    In order for your Realtor or attorney to work on your behalf, negotiating the transaction, you have to give them authority to discuss your finances with the lender. If the lender doesn't receive something giving the Realtor or attorney authorization, they simply won't respond.

The letter, like the cover letter, needs to express its purpose, include the loan number and your social security number and specifically provide authorization.

Realtor's Authorization to Release Loan Information (example)

Date: _____

To: _____

_____

Re: Loan # _____ Borrower(s): _____

_____

We, Matt and Susan Reynolds, have the above loan secured against our property at 2625 Happy Hollow Court in Wildwood, New Jersey. We have listed this property for sale with a Realtor, Brent Wilcox of Century 21 Keim Realtors.

We hereby give authority to our Realtor to speak with you with regard to our financial situation and our mortgage, and to release any matters related to this mortgage to the Realtor. We further give authority to our Realtor to negotiate any loan payoff on our behalf.

This authorization expires one year after the above date.

Our Social Security Numbers are:

Name: _____ Social Security No: _____
Name: _____ Social Security No: _____

Sincerely,

_____
Matt Reynolds

_____
Susan Reynolds

Seller's Hardship Letter

    A hardship letter is an explanation of what happened to the borrower that caused them to get into financial distress with the mortgage. This letter should start with a succinct explanation of the situation the home owner is currently in, and then chronologically explain their circumstances from A to Z.

    The goal of the hardship letter is to convince the mortgage company that the home owner's financial hardship is so great they certainly will never be able to correct the situation without some accommodation by the lender.

    If you are the borrower or you are a Realtor assisting a borrower, you need to remember that the lender does not want the home back, and further, the lender does not want the borrower to file bankruptcy and stay in the home, potentially not paying anything to the lender for the next year.

> Dear Mr. Bigmoneylender,
>
> The loan on my home at 2625 Happy Hollow Court in Wildwood, NJ is delinquent and I am unable to keep making mortgage payments. I have been notified that I am in foreclosure. My mortgage delinquencies are due to a job loss, illness, divorce…
>
> I have received an offer on my home, and believe it is a fair offer based on feedback from all the showings I've had while the home was on the market…
>
> My attorney has advised me to file bankruptcy, but I would prefer to work something out with your mortgage company and not have a bankruptcy on my credit.
>
> My home needs significant repairs and I don't have the resources to complete those repairs. They include…
>
> I sincerely hope you'll consider my request for a short sale on my home. You can reach me any time at …
>
> Sincerely,
>
> Matt Reynolds

However, if the lender believes that the borrower has sufficient resources to continue to pay the mortgage, or if the lender believes that the borrower has no real concrete need to sell the home, the mortgage company may reject the short sale request.

With any hardship letter, the borrower should attempt to provide supporting documentation. If the reason the borrower fell behind was a job loss, then a letter from the employer about the layoff or copies of checks from unemployment may be attached to the letter. If the reason had to do with an illness, then medical bills or other associated information may be included.
If there is damage to the home, or some necessary repair such as a roof leak, that should be outlined in the hardship letter as well. Additionally, the letter should describe what other outstanding bills the borrower has and how this negatively impacts their ability to repay.

Hardship Documentation

Copies of documentation related to owner's hardship as outlined in the previous section. These may include:

- Additional liens against the property or against the borrower personally.
- Any disability statements.
- Copies of medical bills.
- Written documentation from a physician.
- Information on any layoff.

- Copies of unemployment checks or letters.
- Copies of divorce filings.
- Estimates of necessary home repairs.
- Anything else that supports the borrower's case.

Seller's Income, Expense and Asset Worksheet

The "Income, Expense and Asset Worksheet" may also be labeled "Borrower's Financial Statement". Two of the more common versions of this form, used by lenders, are the Fannie Mae Form 1020 and the Freddie Mac Borrower Financial Statement Form 1126. An example of the Fannie Mae 1020 form is on the following page. The Freddie Mac 1126 Form is included on the two pages following it. Whichever version you are requested to fill out, remember that this is a critical form that takes time to prepare.

Remember that the lender does not want to foreclose on the home and potentially lose a lot of money in the foreclosure process. However, the lender also does not want to carry the burden of a loss on the home if the borrower has $50,000 in the bank, a second home and an income that allows the borrower to carry the loan forever. In other words, the lender wants to assess the borrower's actual need for a short sale.

If you're a home owner reading this book, please understand that the bank wants to truly analyze your situation. Most banks or lenders are willing to make something work, but they want to share the pain if possible.

As the home owner, you'll have to itemize whatever assets you have, including money in the bank or invested in liquid assets. Don't try to hide anything here, because the lender is also likely to ask for copies of your last three months bank statements to check and make sure you didn't have a lot of money that you suddenly withdrew. If you have money invested in a liquid asset like mutual funds, the lender may find them by comparing your original application for a mortgage with your new income, expense and asset worksheet.

The reasons the lender wants information on your income and expenses is to determine whether or not you can afford to take part of the loss as a personal loan and pay it back over time. Again, don't fudge the numbers because they will be asking for your paystubs and possibly your tax returns to verify your numbers.

BORROWER'S FINANCIAL STATEMENT

			Servicer Loan Number	
Property Address				
Is your home listed for sale? Yes No	Agent's Name:		Agent's Phone Number:	
Borrower Name			Social Security Number	
Mailing Address (#, Street, Apt)				
Mailing Address (City, State, Zip)				
Total number of persons living at this address:			Number of dependents at this address:	
Home Phone:			Work Phone:	
Co-Borrower Name			Social Security Number	
Mailing Address (#, Street, Apt)				
Mailing Address (City, State, Zip)				
Total number of persons living at this address:			Number of dependents at this address:	
Home Phone:			Work Phone:	
Have you contacted credit counseling services? Yes No			Number of cars you own?	
Monthly Income (Wages): $	/ mo. Additional income (not wages): $		/mo.* Source:	
*Notice: Alimony, child support or separate maintenance income need not be revealed if the Borrower or Co-Borrower does not choose to have it considered for approval of				

Asset Type	Estimated Value	Liability Type	Payment/Month	Balance Due
Home		Alimony/Child Support		
Other Real Estate		Dependent Care		
Checking Accounts		Rent		
Savings/Money Market		Other Mortgage(s)		
IRA/Keogh Accounts		Personal Loan(s)		
401 k/ESOP Accounts		Medical Expenses		
Stocks, Bonds, CD's		HOA Fees/Dues		
Other Investments		Other		
Reason for delinquency:				

I (we) agree that the financial information provided is an accurate statement of my (our) financial status. I (we) understand and acknowledge that any action taken by the lender of my (our) mortgage loan on my (our) behalf will be made in strict reliance on the financial Information provided. My (Our) signature(s) below grants the holder of my (our) mortgage the authority to confirm the information I (we have disclosed in this financial statement, to verify that it is accurate by ordering a credit report, and to contact my real estate agent and/or credit counseling service representative (if applicable).

Submitted this _____ day of _____

By: _____ Date: _____
　　Signature of Borrower

By: _____ Date: _____
　　Signature of Co-Borrower

Before mailing, make sure you have signed and dated the form and attached a copy of your most recent paystub.
If you are self-employed, attached a copy of your most recent Federal Tax returns.

Fannie Mae Form 1020
Jul-06

BORROWER FINANCIAL INFORMATION

Freddie Mac Loan Number _____

BORROWER		CO-BORROWER	
BORROWER'S NAME		CO-BORROWER'S NAME	
SOCIAL SECURITY NUMBER	DATE OF BIRTH	SOCIAL SECURITY NUMBER	DATE OF BIRTH
HOME PHONE NUMBER WITH AREA CODE		HOME PHONE NUMBER WITH AREA CODE	
WORK PHONE NUMBER WITH AREA CODE		WORK PHONE NUMBER WITH AREA CODE	
CELL PHONE NUMBER WITH AREA CODE		CELL PHONE NUMBER WITH AREA CODE	
MAILING ADDRESS			
PROPERTY ADDRESS			

Number of Dependants:	Do you occupy the property? Yes ☐ No ☐	Is it a Rental? Yes ☐ No ☐	
		If yes, please provide copy of lease agreement.	
Is the property listed for sale? Yes ☐ No ☐		Agents name:	
If yes, please provide a copy of the listing agreement.		Agents phone:	
Have you contacted a credit-counseling agency for help?		Counselors Name:	
Yes ☐ No ☐		Counselors Phone:	
Do you pay Real Estate Taxes outside of your mortgage? Yes ☐ No ☐			
If yes, please provide a copy of your tax statement.		Are the taxes current? Yes ☐ No ☐	
Have you filed bankruptcy?	If yes,	Filing Date:	
Yes ☐ No ☐	Chapter 7 ☐ Chapter 13 ☐		
Has your bankruptcy been discharged? Yes ☐ No ☐ If yes, please provide a copy of the discharge paper.			

INVOLUNTARY INABILITY TO PAY

I (We), _____, am/are requesting that the Federal Home Loan Mortgage Corporation (Freddie Mac) review my/our financial situation to determine if I/we qualify for a workout option.

I am having difficulty making my monthly payment because of financial difficulties created by:
(Please check all that apply.)

☐ Abandonment of Property ☐ Excessive Obligation ☐ Military Service
☐ Business Failure ☐ Fraud ☐ Payment Adjustment
☐ Casualty Loss ☐ Illness in Family ☐ Payment Dispute
☐ Curtailment of Income ☐ Illness of Mortgagor ☐ Property Problems
☐ Death in Family ☐ Inability to Rent Property ☐ Title Problems
☐ Death of Mortgagor ☐ Incarceration ☐ Transferring Property
☐ Distant Employment Transfer ☐ Marital Difficulties ☐ Unemployment

I believe that my situation is: ☐ Short term   ☐ Long term   ☐ Permanent

I want to: ☐ Keep my house   ☐ Sell my house

Please provide a detailed explanation of the hardship on a separate sheet of paper.

If there are additional Liens/Mortgages or Judgments on this property, please name the person, company or firm and their respective telephone numbers.

Lien Holder's Name	Balance $	Telephone Number
Lien Holder's Name	Balance $	Telephone Number

Borrower's Signature	Date	Co-Borrower's Signature	Date

Form 1126
1/06

BORROWER FINANCIAL INFORMATION – Page 2

Freddie Mac Loan Number _____

EMPLOYMENT

EMPLOYER - BORROWER	HOW LONG?	EMPLOYER - CO-BORROWER	HOW LONG?

Monthly Income - Borrower		Monthly Income - Co-Borrower	
Wages	$	Wages	$
Unemployment Income	$	Unemployment Income	$
Child Support / Alimony	$	Child Support / Alimony	$
Disability Income	$	Disability Income	$
Rents Received	$	Rents Received	$
Other	$	Other	$
Less : Federal and State Tax, FICA	$	Less : Federal and State Tax, FICA	$
Less: Other Deductions (401K, etc.)	$	Less: Other Deductions (401K, etc.)	$

* * * * * * ALL INCOME NEEDS TO BE DOCUMENTED * * * * * *

	Total	$		Total	$
Monthly Expenses			Assets		
Other Mortgages / Liens	$		Type		Estimated Value
Auto Loan(s)	$		Checking Account(s)		$
Auto Expenses / Insurance	$		Saving / Money Market		$
Credit Cards / Installment Loan(s)	$		Stocks / Bonds / CDs		$
Health Insurance	$		IRA / Keogh Accounts		$
Medical	$		401k / ESPO Accounts		$
Child Care / Support / Alimony	$		Home		$
Food / Spending Money	$		Other Real Estate	#	$
Water / Sewer / Utilities / Phone	$		Cars	#	$
Other	$		Other		$
Total	$			Total	$

"I agree as follows: My lender may discuss, obtain and share information about my mortgage and personal financial situation with third parties such as purchasers, real estate brokers, insurers, financial institutions, creditors and credit bureaus. Discussions and negotiations of a possible foreclosure alternative will not constitute a waiver of or defense to my lender's right to commence or continue any foreclosure or other collection action, and an alternative to foreclosure will be provided only if an agreement has been approved in writing by my lender. The information herein is an accurate statement of my financial status."

Submitted this _____ day of _____, 200____

By _____
    Signature of Borrower

By _____
    Signature of Co-Borrower
    Before mailing, make sure you have signed and dated the form and attached appropriate documentation.

Form 1126
1/05

W-2 Forms for Past Two Years

These are typically requested by lenders considering a short sale in order to determine the borrower's historical income. The lender wants to insure they weren't defrauded when the loan was originally written, and they want to determine if the borrower is currently working significantly below their ability to earn money.

Two Months Pay Stubs

Pay stubs are required to verify the true income of the borrowers. These are required so the borrower doesn't fudge their income, claiming they can't afford the current mortgage. The lender can then make their own determination, based on the borrower's expense report and their current income, whether they can either continue to make mortgage payments. The proof of income also allows the lender to determine whether or not the borrower is likely to be able to handle a personal loan for part of the banks loss in order to mitigate part of that loss.

If there are two borrowers on the mortgage, copies of pay stubs must be provided for each borrower. If there are more than two, obviously, each must provide copies of pay stubs.

If the borrower is self employed, then the lender will require a year-to-date profit and loss statement, which is typically prepared and signed by the borrower's accountant.

Two to Three Months Bank Statements

As with everything else the lender requires, the lender wants to make sure the borrower is really in a desperate situation. The lender's goal is to check for any large withdrawals in the past few months. Perhaps the borrower is trying to walk away from the home, but has assets that could be used to pay part of the loss.

Agreement of Sale or Contract to Purchase the Property

The lender is overwhelmed with requests for short sales, forbearance and repayment plans. They do not want to take the time to negotiate until they have all the facts, and those facts include the market value based on what a buyer is willing to pay. As I stated in the prior section of this book, request a short sale package as early as possible and put together as much information for the lender as you can prior to receiving an offer. Once you have the offer, you can finalize the package and get it into the appropriate hands quickly.

Realtor's Competitive Market Analysis

In order for the lender to accept your offer of a short sale, they are likely to require either a full appraisal of the home, or a Broker's Price Opinion (BPO) of home in order to have an impartial analysis of the likely sales price if they foreclose rather than accept the owner's proposal.

As a quick aside, every time I even mention the term "Broker's Price Opinion", I get mail, email, letter bombs, and so on from appraisers and brokers who emphatically tell me that real estate agents and brokers are prohibited from doing any evaluation of a property that is beyond the scope of simply listing the property for sale. There are brokers and agents on the other side of the issue that believe it is perfectly acceptable to write a value determination for a property without an appraisal license.

I am not taking a position here on whether or not a broker is qualified to evaluate the property for a lender. I'm simply pointing out that it is done regularly across the country, and that in the case of a short sale, a lender will either have a BPO done or an appraisal done.

Whether you are a Realtor attempting to assist a home owner with the short sale process or a home owner doing it yourself, you'll want to provide your own evaluation of the likely sales price of the property. The Realtor selling the property can provide a Competitive Market Analysis or CMA to the lender with the short sale package in order to show the value as determined by the Realtor. In some cases, the lender will accept this CMA and forgo ordering a BPO. In other cases, the CMA will provide additional proof to the lender that the short sale deal is a good one.

Like an appraisal, a Competitive Market Analysis is an evaluation of the home done by comparing the home with recently sold properties that are very similar to it. A CMA, however, also shows the competing properties that are for sale during the same time period. This gives an indication of how likely the home is to sell quickly in the current market based on the competition.

Photos of the home (interior and exterior)

Although I think this should be self explanatory, I want to spell everything out. The lender is unlikely to be in the same home town or state as the property. In these days of megabanks, your home may be in New Jersey and the lender may be in California. The workout department at the bank or mortgage company is trying to understand your situation and your home.

You or your Realtor should include photos of the front and rear of the home, and a street scene to show the surrounding area. You should also include a photo of each room in the home. I recommend you also include a specific photo of every problem area in the home, or any damage to the home along with notes for the photo.

Seller's Net Sheet

A seller's net sheet is an estimation of how much the lender will receive based on the offer being submitted with the package. Any costs or fees the home owner needs to pay in order to settle the property must be included in this net sheet. If you are requesting a short sale, the effect will be that the number at the bottom of the page will be negative. This net sheet can be written by your Realtor. The lender may also require a "preliminary HUD 1" form, which will be discussed in the next heading. Closing costs vary from location to location, including transfer taxes, so the following is for example purposes only.

Seller's Net Sheet: (example)

Sales Price: $200,000

Closing Costs:
  Commission: $ 12,000
  Transfer Tax: $ 2,000
  Notary Fees: $ 50
  Deed Preparation: $ 75
Total Closing Costs: $ 14,125

Mortgages:
  1st Mortgage: $180,000
  Equity Loan: $ 22,000
Total Mortgages: $202,000

Net after Expenses: ($16,125)

Seller is short approximately $16,125 without any additional late fees.

Preliminary HUD 1 Settlement Sheet

Some lenders will not simply accept a Seller's Net Sheet and require the borrower or Realtor to obtain a formal settlement statement from an attorney, title insurance company or escrow company, depending on where in the country you are located. The preliminary HUD statement is done by a third party who is familiar with settlements in order to insure to the title company that no fees are missed.

Payoff Statements for Other Lenders

Many home owners that are under water in their mortgages have additional equity loans, second mortgages or other liens against the property. In order to deliver clear title and settle on your property, these liens or mortgages must also be satisfied or the lenders must agree to accept a short payoff.

Each lender will want proof of the other liens and mortgages in order to determine what they are willing to negotiate. If there are also IRS liens against the property or unemployment compensation liens, they will need to be included and considered as well.

Step 5: Start Calling the Lender!

Remember that there are many people in the same situation across the nation. Lenders are swamped with phone calls and packages. When you complete the package, call and email the lender to determine the best method to get the package to the lender. My suggestion is to send it to them in two forms.

If the lender tells you they'd like the physical package by mail, then I would express the package in order to insure the package gets to the lender quickly and in order to insure it is delivered and can be tracked by who signed for it. I would additionally scan the entire package and email it to the same person to whom you expressed the package.

My goal is to insure they have the package and can begin working on it. If the lender asks the information to be faxed, which some are now doing, I would again both fax it and email it.

Make sure they have the package

You package is going to go onto some pile somewhere and be processed some time in the future, depending on how busy the staff is in the workout or loss mitigation department. As of the writing of this book, one major lender has told us they are taking 90 days to provide any response.

At this point, if you simply wait for something to happen, it may not. The lender may push other files ahead of yours, may lose the file, or may claim they never received it. You'll need to regularly communicate with your contact at the lender's office. If you are a Realtor assisting home owners, set aside some time twice a week to call lenders and determine the package status.

The Appraisal or BPO

As mentioned earlier, lenders often have an appraisal done to determine the current market value of the home. An alternative might be a Broker Price Opinion done by a local real estate broker. In either case, if someone sets up an appointment to view your home on behalf of the bank, you'll want to be prepared to offer two items for their review.

First, remember that this individual is working to evaluate the true market value of the property. In order to get your short sale approved, you want to insure the appraiser or broker understands what is wrong with the property. Provide him or her with a copy of the Competitive Market Analysis done by your Realtor to show what value you believe the home has in the current market.

Secondly, make sure you provide information on any necessary repairs. If the appraiser or broker doesn't know what's wrong with the home, they may not account for it in their evaluation, setting an unrealistically high expectation for the sales price.

The lender may charge you for the appraisal or BPO. In this case, the person evaluating the home may request a check or cash before entering the property. You may be short on funds, but it is important to the process to make sure the evaluation proceeds.

As an additional note, you may be reading more than just this one book about getting a home sold when the borrower owes more than the market will bear. Some investment books explain to home owners that they won't get anything out of the home, so they should set a very low price and at least give some equity to the buyer. They should then try to persuade the appraiser to reduce the appraisal by delivering a high powered sob story directly to the appraiser. I'm always shocked when I read this, but I've seen it several times. The appraiser or broker is trying to do an honest evaluation. Don't try to pressure them to commit fraud on your behalf. Give them the facts and sell the home for a fair value.

Expect a Counter Proposal

Hopefully the lender will simply accept the short sale proposal as written and allow the sale to be consummated. Don't be surprised if the lender refuses the initial offer and makes a counter proposal. Should this happen, you may have to go back to the buyer and ask for more money in order to settle the transaction.

If you are a Realtor, you should be preparing your buyers to understand that this is a negotiation. The lender may accept the deal, or may counter.

What if there's more than one mortgage?

Many home owners are facing the difficulty of dealing with more than one mortgage on their home. In order to transfer the property to a new owner, all liens and mortgages against the property have to be satisfied or released. Whether you are the Realtor assisting the home owner, or you are the home owner, you'll need to negotiate with all parties to complete the short sale.

Negotiating with two or three lenders, rather than one, seems like a daunting task. After all, it took you two and a half hours just to get the first one on the phone. There is a bright side, however. Second and third lien holders, whether they are equity loans, second mortgages or any other liens, typically receive little or nothing if the home is foreclosed by the primary lender. This simple fact may make the lenders more receptive to significantly reduced payoffs.

When a foreclosure sale or Sheriff's sale occurs, the property is sold to the highest bidder. Many homes that go to foreclosure do so because the owner's owe more than the home can be sold for in the current market. The holder of the first mortgage or principal mortgage will typically bid on the home as high as the balance on the first mortgage or as high as the amount the mortgage holder believes they can sell the property for, whichever is lower. Lenders bid in this manner in order to recoup the maximum they can from the property.

In many cases, the bid from the first mortgage company or primary lien holder is the highest or winning bid. A Sheriff's Deed or Trustee's Deed is filed to deed the property back to the winning bidder, and the loans are all extinguished from the title. This leads to home equity loans and second mortgages receiving little or nothing from the foreclosure sale.

Example 1: Property is foreclosed by lender. There is a first mortgage of $180,000 and a second mortgage of $35,000. The lender believes the property may be resold for $200,000. The lender will bid up to $180,000 to insure their loan is repaid through the sale. If others bid above $180,000, the balance is paid to the junior lien holders and then to the owner in that order. If the primary lender is the high bid, the junior lien holders get nothing.

Property Value:	$200,000
1st Mortgage:	$180,000
2nd Mortgage:	$35,000
Total Owed:	$215,000

Primary lender may bid to $180,000. If the primary lender buys the property back at $180,000, the junior lien holders (second mortgage, home equity loans) get nothing from the sale.

Example 2: Property is foreclosed by lender. There is a first mortgage of $225,000 and a second mortgage of $50,000. The lender believes the property may be resold for $200,000. The lender is likely to bid up to $200,000 to insure their loan is repaid through the sale. Even if others bid above $200,000, the first lien holder receives the first

$225,000, leaving the junior lien holders receiving little or nothing.

Property Value:	$200,000
1st Mortgage:	$225,000
2nd Mortgage:	$ 50,000
Total Owed:	$275,000

Primary lender may bid to $200,000. If the primary lender buys the property back at $200,000, the junior lien holders (second mortgage, home equity loans) get nothing from the sale.

    The existence of second and third lien holders may make the negotiation with the first lien holder more difficult because the first mortgage company may believe that they can recoup their entire mortgage in the foreclosure process. All the losses of the short sale may have to be carried by the second mortgage company or any other junior lien holders.

    As with any negotiation, the home owner must be prepared to understand that the first mortgage company may reject the offer of a short sale if they believe they can do better through the process of foreclosure. If you, dear reader, are a Realtor advising clients, you must make the client aware of this possibility.

Negotiating with Junior Liens

There are three possible options to deal with junior liens. Again, we're defining junior liens as second mortgages, third mortgages, home equity loans or any other lien behind the primary mortgage on the property.

The first method of dealing with junior liens only applies if the lien is a piggyback loan. A piggyback loan is a second mortgage written by the same lender as the first mortgage or primary mortgage. With piggyback loans, a Realtor or home owner may be able to negotiate with one single mortgage workout person. In some cases, the lender may still have different people work on either loan.

The piggyback loan allows the lender to spread the shortage of payoff over both loans. This allocation of the payoff may allow the lender some benefits on their books.

The second method is to simply negotiate a short payoff, as described under the previous section of the short sale process. The second lien holder will likely have all the same required documentation as the first. This mortgage company will want to see exactly how much they'll be receiving from the sale based on a preliminary HUD settlement sheet from a title company, attorney or escrow agent.

Remember when dealing with the second mortgage holder that they are likely to lose the entire loan if the owner defaults and goes to foreclosure. That may allow you as either the Realtor or owner to negotiate a payoff that is a fraction of what is owed on the loan. The recourse the second mortgage holder has, however, is the possibility of filing a deficiency judgment should the property go to foreclosure, depending on location and applicable laws.

In order to settle a property with a first and second mortgage, the lender needs to understand their bottom line at the end of the transaction. Assuming the sales price is within an acceptable range of the market value, the first mortgage and closing costs to settle must be paid at settlement. The second mortgage holder must be willing to accept what is left as payment for the lien in order for the borrower to close the loan under this scenario.

Example: A home is valued at $200,000 and receives an offer of $200,000. In order to settle the property, closing costs are $13,000 including Realtor fees, transfer taxes, notary and filing fees. An outstanding first mortgage of $170,000 exists and the second mortgage is $50,000.

Sales Price:	$200,000
Closing Costs:	($ 13,000)
First Mortgage:	($170,000)
Balance:	$ 17,000

In this scenario, the second place mortgage company must be willing to accept $17,000 in lieu of the $50,000 balance on their loan. As with any short sale, an owner should get something in writing from the lender stating that they are accepting this payoff as payment in full for the loan, and that the lender will not pursue civil action for any balance at a later time.

If the lender is unwilling to release the lien at an amount equal to what is left after the first mortgage is paid, as shown in the example above, the alternative is for the home owner to accept a personal note for the difference. At this point, the home owner can elect to file bankruptcy or allow the property to foreclose, but should give serious consideration to their situation.

Getting to Settlement

As with any transaction, title insurance must be ordered and settlement must be scheduled. In instances where an owner may be behind on their mortgage or may be considering a short sale, a wise move for either the Realtor or home owner would be to contact an attorney, title agent or escrow company to run a preliminary title search of the property. Make sure there are no other liens against the property.
Once a lender agrees to accept a short payoff, the owner needs to be ready to move quickly to complete the transaction.

Chapter 5: Realtor's guide to growing their business through short sales

Realtors across the country are making a great living in a depressed market by concentrating on assisting struggling home owners through the short sale process. Although it's a complex process that takes a lot of time, it can also be a very lucrative business in the current climate.

There is a risk, however, in working with home owners to facilitate short sales. You must be careful to disclose all of the owner's options to them, or risk the home owner coming back after you at a later date, claiming they may have done better by using an alterative to a short sale.

Benefits for working short sales

A common declaration I hear from agents after their first short sale is *"Wow, these are a lot of work. I'm never doing one again."* The other comment is *"Why wouldn't I just sell regular homes. They're a lot less work."*

One of the primary reasons that short sales are beneficial to the Realtor is that the home owner's are motivated to sell, and are willing to price the property appropriately for the market in order to avoid foreclosure or further damage to their credit. Additionally, buyers are interested in short sales because they may be buying the homes at a discount.

Realtor's Benefits from working with Short Sales

More Listings

Motivated Sellers

Referrals from Sellers you assist

More Buyers generated from advertising "Short Sale"

There are many other reasons that short sales can help drive your real estate business to great heights. The fact that you are actively pursuing short sale listings leads to an increase in your personal listing inventory of potentially saleable listings. This increased inventory leads to more buyers contacting you to view the properties, which potentially leads to more sales, even if the buyers don't purchase the specific property they call about. In fact, my team has found that if you advertise "Short Sale Home", the number of calls on the property increases because the perception of buyers is that they are buying at a low price.

Further, if you treat the home owner well, and work hard on their behalf, they will reward you with referrals of friends, family members and co-workers who need to buy and sell real estate. You'll also find that your clients will talk about how you assisted them in a tough situation, which will lead to referrals from unexpected sources.

Challenges of working with short sales

There are a similar number of challenges when working to assist home owners in their struggle to sell the home before the foreclosure sale. Of course, the biggest challenge is the sheer time it can take to contact the lender and negotiate on behalf of the home owner.

To further complicate matters, you may spend many hours trying to put a short sale together, only to have it implode at the last minute and net you absolutely nothing in commission. However, in a real estate market where lenders are changing mortgage programs continually, appraisers are being over cautious and buyers are jittery, the chance of getting to settlement on any property is reduced regardless of whether or not it is a short sale situation.

Another challenge you must be aware of is the risk of giving a home owner bad advice and opening yourself and your company to a potential lawsuit for

---

Realtor's Challenges when working with Short Sales

Reduced Commissions

Time spent talking to lender

Risk of suit for poor advice

The chance that the lender will simply refuse the short sale damages. Be absolutely certain to disclose to your clients that they have the right and opportunity to speak with an attorney, accountant and any other professional they would like. Additionally, have the home owner sign a release that specifically spells out the different options that *may* be available to them, and authorizes you to work on their behalf. A sample of this will be included later in this chapter.

The final major negative to working with short sales is the chance that the lender will only agree to accept the short sale if you agree to reduce your commission. The lender may want to "share the pain". While some trainers advocate holding firm and refusing to negotiate because they believe the lender will give in, I've found this tactic more often antagonizes the lender and may lead to a lost deal.

Prospecting for Short Sales

In the book *"Real Estate Prospecting: The Ultimate Resource Guide"*, I explain various methods of targeting a particular audience for your message, determining the correct message to send and finding the best way to deliver that message.[v] In my opinion, prospecting is not simply sending out a letter once in a while. For you to build a solid and successful career in the real estate field, you need to understand that prospecting needs to be a system that consistently communicates with your desired target market. Successful prospecting is a system, not an event.

When working with home owners who are likely to sell through the process of a short sale, you have several ways to find them. First, you can directly locate those people who are already so far behind on their mortgages that the lender has filed a foreclosure action against them. Second, you can advertise in a variety of media that you are assisting home owners that need help with the process. You may even find that writing an article for the local paper about the short sale process can bring you potential clients.

Finally, you can spread the word about your experience working with short sales by communicating to your sphere of influence and your past clients that you can and will help customers in need of this kind of assistance. It seems that everyone knows someone who is having difficulty with their mortgage. A strong word-of-mouth campaign can bring in many potential customers.

Prospecting at the Courthouse

If a home owner has a foreclosure action filed against them, they are strong candidates for a short sale. Although time is often short once a foreclosure action is filed, the home owner may be far more willing to do whatever it takes to keep the foreclosure off their credit, and may be in a strong position to listen to alternatives.

Foreclosure court actions are a matter of public record and will be available for review. Find out where, in your county, those records can be viewed and start looking at them regularly. Keep a list, and begin mailing, calling or stopping by those homes that are in jeopardy of foreclosure to explain how you may be able to help them.

The objective in contacting any prospective client is to get them to work with you. Your initial contact is likely to be made simply in order to secure an appointment to meet with the prospective client in person or by phone in order to explain your services and hopefully secure a listing contract.

The challenge is how to make your voice heard by these potential customers over the noise of all the other calls and letters they're receiving. If you're attempting to mail to this group, you should be aware that mail has a very low response rate, and worse, they are receiving lots of mail from other groups contacting them about their situation. When a foreclosure action is made a matter of public record, the home owner will be contacted by attorneys who want to assist the home owner in filing bankruptcy, investors looking for a deal, and others looking to benefit from the home owner's situation.

If you choose to prospect by calling these home owners, you'll have to be aware that they are likely to be receiving many harassing calls from the lenders. If they are not paying their mortgage, they may also be late in paying other creditors like utility companies, credit card companies and the like. These home owners may even be screening all calls in order to avoid the harassing phone calls.

My suggestion is to use a combination of contact methods including mailings and phone calls or personal visits. Personal contact is always most effective in obtaining an appointment to explain your services, but it is not always possible. From my experience, those agents who are the most successful in contacting home owners in a foreclosure situation are those that either call or door knock those owners.

When I'm giving a live speech or workshop and I introduce the idea of calling or door knocking, Realtors stick up their hands to announce that they've determined they can contact many more people by mailing them all the same information. The problem is that mailings have a very low success rate. You may send out several hundred mailing pieces without a single response. In fact, many people open their mail over the garbage can in order to throw away anything that looks even remotely like an advertising piece.

If you are absolutely terrified of making calls or knocking on doors, you may be limited to the poor results of mailing, or you may need to team up with someone who is willing to personally contact potential clients, or you may need to change your career.

If you ultimately decide to prospect by mail despite my warnings, what should you send these potential clients? What will bring the highest number of responses? Remember that these prospective clients are already receiving a lot of mail. Your information needs to stand out from the rest. One method is to create a simple postcard piece that highlights your service. Although a postcard is an obvious marketing piece, a postcard is also something that doesn't need to be opened to be read.

> ## Are you facing foreclosure? We may be able to help!
>
> Our real estate team assists home owners in this area to negotiate with lenders to allow the home to be sold at a fraction of the amount owed to get you out from under the mortgage with no foreclosure, no bankruptcy, and no further obligations to your lender.
> This process is called a Short Sale.
>
> Please let us help you! Call us for details…
> **Sign of the Bat Realty**
> **800-000-0000**

When planning any mailing or advertising, consider that most of the effectiveness of the marketing is in the headline. If the reader isn't enticed by the headline, they won't read the rest of the message. Try testing different headlines for your area and review the results to determine which are most effective in generating leads.

Don't stop at one postcard to each client. You should attempt several different approaches until you receive a call from the client. A second may be a professional looking letter.

Are you facing foreclosure? We may be able to help WITHOUT Bankruptcy!

Dear Home Owner,

Our real estate team assists home owners in this area to negotiate with their lenders, often allowing the home to be sold at a fraction of the amount owed, in order to get you out from under the mortgage with no foreclosure, no bankruptcy, and no further obligations to your lender. This process is called a Short Sale.

For example, recently we assisted a couple that owed $315,000 on their 4 bedroom Parkland colonial and were in danger of foreclosure. In the current market, the home could only be sold for $290,000. We assisted them in negotiating with the mortgage company to take a "short payoff". The mortgage company paid all closing costs and cleared the mortgage. The home owner was able to move without owing a dime and their credit is much better as a result of avoiding foreclosure.

If you, or someone you know, is in a similar situation, please let us help. Call me, **Joe Bartera** at **Fun with Cats Realty**, at 800-000-0000 and ask for me by name.

Sincerely,

Joe Bartera

PS – Call for a copy of our free report "How to Avoid Foreclosure by Negotiating a Short Sale with your Lender". This informative report is yours with no obligation. Simply call and we'll mail or email it to you.

The sample letter above includes a story that will hopefully resonate with the home owner. Here is an example of another family in the same trouble, and you were able to assist them in resolving the issue. This type of letter provides evidence of your success and will dramatically increase the responses you will receive from any mailing.

The second component of this letter that attracts attention is the postscript. It is the offer of a free report. Free information, with no obligation or strings attached, attracts potential clients who aren't ready to meet with a "salesperson", but want to know their rights and their options. When someone calls you for a copy of this report, they are raising their hand and telling you that they are in the market for assistance.

Simply put together a three or four page explanation of the short sale process and have it ready, along with your information on every page, to send out to potential clients who request it. Once you've identified the most likely clients, you can begin more aggressively following up with mail or possibly phone calls. We'll cover this further in a section on follow-up.

Cold Calling Clients

I hear a rush of inhaled breath every time I use the dreaded words "Cold Call", but the truth is that it is one of the most effective methods of prospecting for potential clients. Simply pick up the phone and call those people who need your services. Keep in mind that you may be helping the property owner by getting them out of a very difficult situation that is fraught with stress and emotion.

"But, Loren – we're not allowed to call anyone anymore. Haven't you heard of the Do Not Call List?" Cross reference the list and don't call those you're not permitted to call. Again, there are plenty of people who are not part of the do not call list. If too many people on your list of prospective short sale owners are part of the 'Do Not Call' list, then you may have to resort to door knocking.

I've always believed that a simple and direct script works best. Practice what you're going to say by yourself and then with a partner before making your first call. But don't hesitate when the time comes. Make that call! An example is:

Realtor: *"Hi, Mrs.Arbegast?"*

Home Owner: *"Yes?"*

Realtor: *" This is Simon Bonaparte calling from Century 21 At Your Service Realty. I'm just calling because I noticed your home was listed on the most recent foreclosure list from the courthouse. I specialize in assisting home owners in that situation to negotiate short sales with their lenders to try to get the home owner out of the home without a foreclosure or bankruptcy on their credit. I do this at no cost* to you because my fees are paid by the bank. Are you considering selling the home in order to get out from under the mortgage?"

If the home owner you're speaking with asks questions, but does not set up an appointment with you, you still have a good potential lead. Make sure to follow-up with a Personal Note Card and thank them for being so pleasant on the phone.

Advertising for Clients

For those potential clients who are good short sale candidates, but are not yet at the point of having a foreclosure filed, there is no easy way to directly identify them. In order to attract these home owners, you'll need to advertise. Advertising can take many forms, including both online and offline.
In either form, you'll need to find a way to entice them to contact you. Online sources of free advertising include Craig's list and any local free classified services. Print advertising includes your local newspaper and perhaps a small box ad in the local real estate magazine.

Are you facing foreclosure? We may be able to help!

Our real estate team assists home owners in this area to negotiate with lenders to allow the home to be sold at a fraction of the amount owed to get you out from under the mortgage with no foreclosure, no bankruptcy, and no further obligations to your lender. This process is called a Short Sale.

Please let us help you!
Call us for details…
Guinevere and Lancelot
Round Table Realtors
800-ART-HUR1

Or call for a copy of our free report "How to Avoid Foreclosure by Negotiating a Short Sale with your Lender". This informative report is yours with no obligation. Simply call and we'll mail or email it to you.

> # Mortgage Trouble?
> # Our local real estate team assists home owners with negotiating short sales with lenders!
>
> Our real estate team assists home owners in this area to negotiate with lenders to allow the home to be sold at a fraction of the amount owed to get you out from under the mortgage with no foreclosure, no bankruptcy, and no further obligations to your lender. This process is called a Short Sale.
>
> Please let us help you! Call us for details…
> Absolute Realty
>
> Or call for a copy of our free report "How to Avoid Foreclosure by Negotiating a Short Sale with your Lender". This informative report is yours with no obligation. Simply call and we'll mail or email it to you.

Attracting Customers with Workshops

Another great source of potential short sale listings can be created by marketing yourself as the local expert in short sales. One of the best methods of setting yourself apart as the expert is to hold workshops on subjects that would appeal to the group of potential customers in this situation. While hosting a workshop, you are immediately seen as the expert in the field.

The other great benefit of holding a workshop rather than simply advertising for potential clients to call you is that a workshop setting puts the client in a more relaxed frame of mind, because they don't feel the pressure of dealing with a "salesperson" on the phone or in person.

You may even find that you can offset the cost of the workshop by partnering with a mortgage broker or title agent.

Word of Mouth

Hopefully, you already have a successful real estate practice with many past clients and a strong sphere of influence. A short sale program should be an additional tool in your real estate tool belt. It should be one more target market that you concentrate on building for your career.

You can garner additional prospective clients in need of assistance by informing your past clients and sphere of influence about your foray into short sales. Write a letter or email to all of your past clients explaining what a challenge short sales are and how you are currently assisting customers through this challenging process.

Chances are that many of your past clients and sphere of influence already know someone in this situation and may be able to cheerlead for you, bringing you potential clients.

Follow Up

As I mentioned earlier in this chapter, the primary reason for any marketing is to get potential customers to first identify themselves as being in the market to use your services, and secondly to obtain an appointment to do business. In order to be the most effective at capturing those leads and converting them into clients, you need to have a system in place to follow up with the potential clients.

Elbert Hubbard once wrote that *"many a man has thrown up his hands at a time when a little more patience would have achieved success."*[vi] Follow up is critical to your success as a Realtor.

If you don't have your clients organized in some form of electronic database, you need to go get one as quickly as possible. This database may be an online program, such as Top Producer, or it may be a program you purchase and install in your computer, such as ACT.

Unless you have some sort of contact management software, you'll be trying to maintain contact with your clients by hand and will be less able to compete with those agents who are more computer savvy. Any contact management program will have a list of your clients, along with their contact information.

Mailing, e-mailing and phone calls can be rotated to follow-up with clients and keep in touch until they're ready to meet with you to discuss your services. Have you ever visited a cave or cavern and had the tour guide explain that stalactites and stalagmites are really just mineral deposits from water slowly dripping on one spot over time? Any good contact management program that you purchase and use effectively will accomplish the same task. Over time, you're planting seeds about yourself and your business.

Each contact, whether by mail, phone, e-mail or in person, will help to build your long-term relationship with that person you're contacting. The most important facet of the process is laying out a system and continuing to follow it.

I've found that in my own business, when I get very busy, I forget to send out mailers, newsletters and I stop maintaining contact with my database. My business slowly goes down like a balloon with a slow air leak. When I begin reconnecting with the database, leads re-appear and my business increases.

To avoid this up-and-down cycle, you should plan out any system a minimum of 90 days in advance. If you plan on using a mix of newsletters, e-mails and personal hand written notes, then plan your activities for specific dates over the next 90 days. Write all the newsletters at the same time, if possible, so you simply have to send them or put them in the mail with very little thought.

Testimonial Letters

One of the most effective types of communication a potential client can receive is a third-party endorsement of your service. In other words, if you have a very satisfied client who is willing to write their experiences in a letter to you, you can copy the letter or parts of the letter into a brochure, a mailing or an e-mailing.

If the message is emotionally charged and specifically outlines what you were able to accomplish for the client, your response will be even better. This is particularly true in situations where a prospective client is in significant risk of losing their home, as many short sale candidates are.

Short of receiving an actual testimonial letter, you can create stories based on your experiences and send them out in letter or postcard form. These short stories become evidence of your success as a Realtor.

The Short Sale Listing Appointment

There are two primary keys to successfully working with home sellers. First, you are far more likely to list a property and help the home owners if they both like and trust you. Second, you need to listen carefully to their needs and their concerns so you can directly address them.

In order to help these potential clients to like you and trust your opinion, it's important to position yourself as an expert prior to engaging them at an appointment. Far too often, a home seller will make a snap decision about whether or not they like a Realtor based on what the Realtor looks like standing at the front door. It is hard to recover from that first impression.

You may look like the home owner's old brother-in-law that the home owner can't stand.

My solution for this challenge is to have a package mailed or delivered to the home owner prior to the appointment. Include information on short sales, information on your real estate team and a short biography. Write your own version of the short sale process in a booklet form with your name on the front. Position yourself as the expert.

When you arrive at the home for your appointment, give the home owner a warm and friendly smile and navigate them to the kitchen table. You'll find it much easier to write down numbers and lay out a game plan to avoid foreclosure by sitting at a kitchen table rather than across the living room from one another.

Before touring the home, try to sit down at the table and examine the home owner's situation. This is another method of showing a potential home seller that you care about their needs and concerns. Make sure to go over all required disclosures for your state because you'll be discussing the home owner's finances.

At the starting point of the conversation with home owners, I suggest explaining what you're planning to do and then asking a series of questions to qualify the home owner. There are specific reasons for doing this.

The home owner is obviously nervous and has been given all sorts of advice about what they should do. You want them to value your opinion, and they won't do that until they trust that you're working to do what is in their best interest. You don't want the home owner to believe you are simply there to "get the listing" and put a sign up to attract buyers.

My initial statement for a home owner in this situation is:

"Before we get started, I just want to give you a little background on me. I want you to understand that I am not here just to try to list your home. Most of my business comes from clients who refer me to other clients. My goal is to help you any way I can, because ultimately, if I'm successful in helping you with your situation, you will hopefully help me to grow my business over time by referring me to your friends and relatives. Does that make sense?

Great. Then what I'm going to do is try to better understand your situation so I can determine if and how I can properly assist you. I have a few questions I'd like to run through with you, if that's okay."

There are several reasons to ask a series of questions. First, you truly want to fully understand their situation in order to help them. Second, when you write down the answers, you are showing the home owners that you *do* care about them and their needs and concerns. This will go a long way to helping them like and trust you.

There are many questions you can ask home owners in this situation. The few that I normally ask include:

1. How long have you been thinking about potentially selling the home?

2. Are you currently in foreclosure on the home?

3. How long do you have before the Sheriff Sale?

4. Do you have more than one mortgage against the property?

5. Do you have any home equity loans or IRS liens that could have been placed against the property?

6. Have you tried talking to your lender (or lenders) about a short sale yet?

7. Do you have an idea of how much you currently owe on each loan?

8. What kind of financial situation are you currently experiencing? I need to understand your complete situation in order to negotiate for you.

Answering the Home Owner's Objections

When dealing with home owners who are in jeopardy of foreclosure, you'll find many that are more willing to listen to your honest opinion of price than typical home sellers. However, you'll also find many that have difficulty truly understanding their situation.

One of the most common concerns I hear is that the home owner won't sell unless they get some sort of cash out of the transaction in order to move. I can tell you from experience that it almost never happens that a lender will allow the seller to walk away with a dime from the table.

In one case a few years ago, a couple called me only weeks before the Sheriff's sale. The time was rapidly approaching when the couple would be physically removed from their home. In this type of case, the owners had no time to wait for the highest price.

The market was slow and the average market time was in excess of 90 days. The couple had less than 30 to move out of the property. I explained to them that we needed to price the home below market in order to get it sold in time. The wife, who we'll call Mrs. O, was very irate that I would even suggest such a thing when they needed every penny they could get out of the house to pay off their debt. I explained to her, to the best of my ability as I have to many home owners over time, that a home's sales price is a function of time.

If you have all the time in the world, you may get a higher price. In a world with no time constraints, you may find that perfect buyer who'll pay the most money for it, but if you need to sell in a short period of time you may have to sell at a wholesale price or below market price in order to attract a buyer to buy your house over someone else's.

If we know that we've only got weeks to sell a house, and there are 50 or 60 other houses on the market competing with it, and only two or three of them will sell in those few weeks, we have to make sure ours is the most attractive in the market place in order to get it sold. After much discussion, we priced the house 10% below market in order to get a quick sale, and we started an aggressive marketing campaign to try to get anyone humanly possible into the home before the date that they would lose the home.

This can be a tough thing for home owners to hear, but they need to understand that our goal is to get them out of the foreclosure process so they don't have it on their credit.

The second common question from home owners in this situation is *"Why should I even bother putting in the time and effort to try to get a short sale? My credit is already ruined and I just want those phone calls from the mortgage company to stop. I'd rather just walk away."*

Many of these home owners are behind on more than just their mortgages. They could be at risk of losing their car and behind in utility and credit card bills. They believe their credit will never be good enough to borrow again, so why bother?

The reality is that credit can be fixed over time. With good explanations and carefully maintaining good credit once their home is sold, they'll have a good chance of reestablishing their credit. They can even work with agencies to help them. The first step is to get out from under that mortgage without having a foreclosure.

Although their credit may be significantly damaged, a foreclosure or bankruptcy can be far worse for far longer than simply being behind on credit cards and utility bills. The foreclosure or bankruptcy will stay on their credit for seven to ten years.

They should consider their situation carefully. Perhaps they're right and they'll never be able to purchase a home again, but chances are they'll eventually need a car loan. Their credit score will affect the interest rate they pay for credit cards, and any other long term payment plans they attempt to set up.

Another issue is that their credit will even affect where they live. We've had dozens of clients with foreclosures and bankruptcies apply to rent homes. The property owner's first question to us is *"If they couldn't afford a mortgage, how are they going to afford to pay my rent? They had something invested in their home and they lost it. They have nothing invested in my rental property."* These clients may ultimately be turned down by many landlords because of the credit issues.

Remember that you have to be very careful not to give advice for which you are not educated or licensed. The client should be referred to credit counseling, a lawyer or an accountant, but you should be aware that these people need assistance.

Another common question by home owners is whether or not they can apply for a short sale when they are not currently behind in their mortgage. One of my biggest frustrations is that too many Realtors are answering "yes" to this question. The answer is "no"! In the past, most lenders didn't want to discuss the possibility of a short sale unless they were worried the borrower was in imminent default. Most have now come to realize that it is in their best interest to negotiate earlier before the client begins missing payments because the clients are more likely to walk away and stick the bank with six months to a year of missed payments and the ultimate cost of foreclosure. You do not have to be in foreclosure or missing payments in order to negotiate for a short sale.

    A fourth question that pops up regularly is whether or not the property has to be "approved" for a short sale prior to marketing. As we outlined earlier in the book, the vast majority of lenders will not approve any sort of short sale without an offer. You must market the home, find a buyer and then begin negotiating. Price the home appropriate for the market, disclosing that it is subject to short sale or bank approval, in order to attract buyers and negotiate from that point.

    A fifth concern of home sellers is if they have enough time to market the home and get a short sale approved. You'll have to determine the foreclosure time frame for your particular area, but in most of the country, the foreclosure process takes six months to a year. The short sale approval process may take thirty days to ninety days. Often, if you have an offer, you can additionally stall the Sheriff's Sale by communicating with the lender.

"What if I have both a first and second mortgage?" many home owners ask. This is a common problem in the current market. Both lenders will have to be satisfied in one way or another and both will have to approve the short sale. Go back and read chapter 4 for more information.

Finally, a common concern of home sellers is who will pay the closing costs? After all, the home owner owes more than the home can be sold for in the current market. When a short sale is processed, the bank or lender is looking at the bottom line, after closing costs. Effectively, the lender pays the commission, transfer taxes and other closing costs out of their proceeds at settlement. If the owner is upside down in their mortgage and a short sale is approved, those costs come out of the transaction, so that the home owner won't have to bring money to settlement.

Protecting Yourself with Disclosures

As I've repeated throughout this book, have an attorney review anything. This is also applicable to real estate agents and brokers who want to protect themselves. Our disclosure is an example. Each state is different and laws are constantly changing. Make sure you have an attorney put together a disclosure to protect you.

One critical component of protecting yourself is to be certain the home owner is aware of all possible choices that they can make, including methods of renegotiating with their lender to stay in the home. You certainly don't want to be sued after settlement by a former home owner who claims that you told them their only option was to sell quickly and below market.

In the first chapter of this book, we went over the seven alternatives or options someone has to avoid foreclosure. Give these options to your prospective client and have them sign that they received information about each.

A sample disclosure statement is outlined on the next page. Have any disclosure you intend to use reviewed by a licensed attorney in your state.

Realtor's Disclosure Statement
Options to avoid foreclosure

Home Owner: _____
Property: _____
Date: _____

We, the undersigned owners, are at risk of foreclosure and have contracted with Century 21 Keim Realtors to market our home for sale. We understand that this sale may be subject to a "short sale" where our lender(s) would have to agree to accept a reduced payoff of their liens.

We have further been made aware of our options to avoid foreclosure, including options of renegotiating the terms of our mortgage with our lender(s) or requesting a forbearance of the payments for a period of time.

The options that have been outlined by the Century 21 Keim Realtor include:

    1. Mortgage Modification
    2. Repayment Plan
    3. Forbearance Agreement
    4. Re-instatement of Mortgage

5. Short Sale
6. The Deed in Lieu of Foreclosure
7. Bankruptcy

We have also been made aware that our Realtor is not an attorney or accountant and have been given a recommendation to speak with a credit counselor, attorney and accountant.

Owners: _____

_____

Summary

Carefully read through all the steps in this book so you understand how best to assist home owners with their short sale needs. You may want to take the time to seek out agents in other parts of the country that have successfully negotiated short sales and ask for their help or advice.

Once you understand the process, begin prospecting for clients, as you would if you were trying to build a business based on any type of property or geographic group or demographic group.

Remember that the real estate market is a moving target. In some markets, luxury properties sell very well. In others, investment properties are the product of choice. With the huge number of foreclosures and home owners in trouble in the current market, short sales are a very lucrative target market for a Realtor.

As I pointed out at the very beginning of this chapter, Realtors across the country are making a great living in a depressed market by concentrating on assisting struggling home owners through the short sale process. It *is* a complex process, and each transaction can take a lot of time, but it can also be a very lucrative business in the current climate.
.

Other Books by Loren Keim
Order online at
www.RealEstatesNextLevel.com

How to Sell Your Home in Any Market: 6 Reasons Why Your Home Isn't Selling... and What You Can Do to Fix Them. (Sphinx Legal)

People sell homes every year in every market throughout the country. However as the market slows down, an owner must compete for fewer buyers in the marketplace. And even when the market is hot, there are still always homes that just don't sell.

The primary reasons why houses don't sell include poor staging, improper pricing, incorrect marketing, functional obsolescence and location challenges (or that people just aren't buying in the area!)

This easy-to-read, well-organized book explains how to fix your house and your sales technique to sell your home faster and for top dollar.

The Fundamentals of Listing and Selling Commercial Real Estate

A complete foundation for a career in the Commercial Real Estate Industry, the text contains a comprehensive study of property and investment analysis, mortgages and leases, as well as practice techniques such as prospecting, presentations, and negotiating.

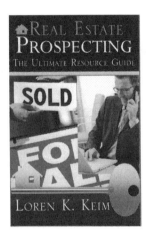

Real Estate Prospecting: The Ultimate Resource Guide

This book is the ultimate game plan for prospecting. It carefully outlines methods to select likely groups of prospects, how to contact those target groups, what to offer them, and how best to follow up.

Loren Keim
Biography

Loren Keim is a national authority on real estate and the housing market.

Keim is the author of several how-to books about real estate, including "How to Sell Your Home in Any Market", "The Fundamentals of Commercial Real Estate" and "Real Estate Prospecting: The Ultimate Resource Guide", and training systems for Realtors. Keim is also the editor-in-chief of Real Estate Investment Digest and Pennsylvania Farm & Ranch Magazine, and is a real estate broker and president of Century 21 Keim Realtors in Pennsylvania.

As an authority on the housing and real estate market, Keim performs an economic analysis and housing projections for Lehigh University's Goodman Center in Bethlehem, PA. Keim has appeared on television and radio programs to talk about the housing market and the recent real estate crisis, and has been a speaker at national conventions.

Keim attended Lehigh University in Bethlehem, PA and entered the field of Real Estate in 1988, quickly becoming one of the top real estate agents in the country with Century 21 Real Estate.

Glossary

A

Agency – The relationship that exists between the sellers of a property and their Realtor or the buyers of a property and their Realtor. This relationship is formed through a written contract that outlines the Realtor's duties and obligations to their client.

C

Capacity - The ability of a borrower to pay back their loan based on a ratio between the borrower's income and the amount of their payments. Lenders carefully determine whether or not the borrower can make the payments by assessing how long the borrower had been employed and what percentage of their income could be used to make the mortgage payment.

Capital - Down money on the purchase of a home. The amount of money a borrower puts down on the home they are purchasing.

Century 21 Keim Realtors – A great real estate company in Eastern Pennsylvania. 800-648-4421.

Closing Costs – Fees that are paid by the buyer or seller in a real estate transaction or paid by a borrower when refinancing their property.

Collateral - The home being borrowed against is the collateral of the loan. The value of the home simply has to be worth what the buyer is paying for it. A lender doesn't want to risk having to take back a property and re-sell it if there isn't enough equity to sell the home in the case of default.

Credit Score – Credit worthiness and determine by a formula and credit history kept by credit reporting agencies such as Transunion and TRW.

Credit Worthiness - History of borrower's credit and payments.

D

Deed in lieu of foreclosure – A borrower's agreement to voluntarily deed their property back to the bank or mortgage company.

Default – When a borrower fails to pay his or her mortgage resulting in the lender filing foreclosure against the property. Default can be used to describe the situation when a buyer or seller fails to follow the terms of the sales contract.

E

Equity – When applied to Real Estate, the term equity refers to the amount of money a property seller may receive after paying off their outstanding mortgages, loans and closing costs to sell.

F

Fannie Mae – The Federal National Mortgage Association (FNMA) is a government sponsored entity that buys mortgages from lenders in order to make mortgage money readily available to home buyers.

Forbearance Agreement - A forbearance agreement is an agreement from the bank or the mortgage company to allow a borrower to delay making mortgage payments for a short period of time.

Foreclosure – The legal process by which a lender takes back a property in return for an outstanding mortgage.

Freddie Mac - A government sponsored entity that buys mortgages from lenders in order to make mortgage money readily available to home buyers.

H

HUD-1 – Also known as a settlement statement or closing statement, the HUD-1 is a document that accounts for all payoffs of liens and closing costs on the settlement of a parcel of real estate.

J

Judicial Sale – A Judicial Sale is a form of foreclosure that is done through the court system.

L

Lender – An entity who loans money.

Lien – A debt against a property that must be satisfied when the property is sold.

M

Mortgage – A legal document that pledges real property as collateral against a loan.

Mortgage Company – An entity that makes a loan with real estate as the collateral.

Mortgage Modification – A modification by the mortgage company to the terms of the mortgage, such as a reduction in interest rate.

O

Owner's Right of Redemption – Some states allow a borrower to redeem the mortgage, affectively buying back the property, for a period after the foreclosure sale. The term of this redemption period varies from state to state but is typically between six months and a year.

P

Power of Sale – A form of foreclosure that is done without the supervision of the court system.

R

Reinstatement of Mortgage - In any state in the country, the borrower has the right to catch up the mortgage prior to the judicial sale, sheriff sale or sale through the power of sale process.

S

Subprime Loan – A loan that is made by a lender that does not conform to normal loan standards. These loans may carry higher-than-average interest rates and are often high risk loans.

.

Index

1

100% financing, 14

A

ACT, 114
Agreement of Sale, 81
Appraisal, 82, 87
Arm's Length Transactions, 63
Attorney, 8

B

Bank Statements, 81
Bankruptcy, 40, 41, 52
Borrower's Financial Statement, 75
BPO, 82
Broker's Price Opinion",, 82

C

Capacity, 13, 135
Capital, 12, 135
Century 21 Keim, 18
Clinton administration, 13
Cold Calling, 107
Collateral., 12, 136
Community Reinvestment Act, 13
Competitive Market Analysis, 81, 82
Contract to Purchase, 81
Cover Letter, 69
Credit Worthiness, 12, 136

D

Database, 113
Declaration of Fair Lending Principals and Practices, 14
Deed in Lieu of Foreclosure, 39, 47
deficiency judgment, 31
Deficiency Judgment, 52
Disclosures, 126

E

Economic crisis, 9
Elbert Hubbard, 113
Evidence of Success, 106, 116

F

fair value legislation, 31
Fannie Mae, 13, 14, 17
Financial Chaos, 9
Follow Up, 113
Forbearance Agreement, 34, 36, 127
Foreclosure, 29
　Judicial Sale, 30
　Power of Sale, 31
　Strict, 29
Freddie Mac, 13, 14
Full Disclosure, 63

G

GSE, 14

H

Hardship Documentation, 74

Hardship Letter, 72
History, 11
Home Ownership, Rate of, 16
Housing Bill, 13
HUD 1, 85

I

Income, Expense and Asset Worksheet, 75

J

Junior Liens, 92

L

Legal advice, 7
Lehigh University, 9
Listing Appointment, 116

M

Marketing the property, 60
medical bills, 74
Mortgage Backed Securities, 21
Mortgage Modification, 34, 35, 127

N

Net Sheet, 83
New York Times, 13

O

Objection Handling, 120
Owner's Right of Redemption, 32

P

Pay Stubs, 80
Payoff Statements, 85
Piggyback Loan, 92
Predatory Lenders, 19
Profit and Loss Statement, 80
Prospecting, 99
  Courthouse, 101
Prospecting, Advertising, 109

R

Realtor's Authorization, 70
Re-instatement of Mortgage, 34, 38, 127
Renting, 45

Repayment Plan, 37

S

Sales Contract Addendum, 66
self employed, 80
Self Employed, 80
Seller's Income, Expense and Asset Worksheet, 75
Settlement Sheet, 85
Seven Options, 32
Short Sale Package, 68, 85
Snow, John, 17
Statutory redemption, 32
Stimulus packages, 11
Strict foreclosure, 29

T

Tax advice, 7
Testimonial Letters, 115
The Deed in Lieu of Foreclosure, 34, 128
Top Producer Software, 114

W

W-2, 80
Wall Street, Rating Agencies, 21

Wilfinger, Robert, 10
Workshops, 111

End Notes

[i] *Peter J Wallison.* **The American Spectator.** Bloomington: Feb 2009. Vol. 42, Iss. 1; pg. 22, 6 pgs

[ii] *Phil Gramm.* **Wall Street Journal.** (Eastern edition). New York, N.Y.; Feb 20, 2009. pg. A.17

[iii] *Phil Gramm.* **Wall Street Journal.** (Eastern edition). New York, N.Y.; Feb 20, 2009. pg. A.17

[iv] *Loren K Keim.* **How to Sell Your Home in Any Market.** 2008. Sphinx Legal / Source Books.

[v] *Loren K. Keim.* **Real Estate Prospecting: The Ultimate Resource Guide.** 2008. Infinity Publishing.

[vi] *Elbert Hubbard.* **The Book of Business.** 1913. The Roycrofters.

Made in the USA